Liberals Don't Flush

Liberals Don't Flush

Barry Mason

iUniverse, Inc.
New York Lincoln Shanghai

Liberals Don't Flush

iUniverse books may be ordered through booksellers or by contacting:

iUniverse
2021 Pine Lake Road, Suite 100
Lincoln, NE 68512
www.iuniverse.com
1-800-Authors (1-800-288-4677)

ISBN-13: 978-0-595-42419-1 (pbk)
ISBN-13: 978-0-595-86754-7 (ebk)
ISBN-10: 0-595-42419-8 (pbk)
ISBN-10: 0-595-86754-5 (ebk)

Printed in the United States of America

Contents

FOREWORD

This book is primarily directed at younger liberals, to assist in their recovery process before it's too late to save them and the errs of their ways become permanent. The pages of this book will no doubt burn liberals' tender fingers. My hope is that they might have a few calluses by the last page. We're all born as liberals after all and must progress from the thick fog of left-wing thought through maturity, progressive responsibility, realism, and hard work. Only by undergoing the natural process of mentally growing up can we expect to someday reach our own individual pinnacles of Conservatism.

The trek toward Conservatism will be fraught with challenges and temptations. The challenges must be accepted and overcome, and the temptations resisted. The road is not a simple one. Many people never complete the journey. Some of them maintain their naïve and underdeveloped thought processes and become stuck in liberalism for life. They age chronologically and physically, but that's about the extent of their development. Heck, some of them even become Presidents!

A child has the right to be a liberal. To be one is expected of a child, just like it's expected of him to mess his drawers, tell lies, throw tantrums, and to look for the good in everyone ... even a terrorist. Oops! Excuse me. I meant the neighborhood bully.

Most children don't have steady jobs. They might do a little chore here and there for an allowance, but they know that there are others far more responsible than they who will provide for them. This is a natural and healthy situation for a child. Many children move into their adult years and never progress beyond this mindset, though. They then qualify for a status change since "child" no longer applies. They can officially be referred to as deadbeats, the poor, welfare recipients, leeches, etcetera. You know ... liberals.

This is not to suggest that all liberals are poor or unsuccessful. I stated before that some even become Presidents. Not only of communist countries, but right here in the good old US of A. Some liberals are successful in business. They can be quite personable. Get into hot issues of debate with them and the shortcomings surface, though.

You may wonder how a liberal could be successful enough to become President if they're as bad as I suggest. I'll get into this later, but the answer in a nutshell is because so many of the American people are cattle. They don't think intricate thoughts or possess intelligent opinions. They just follow. Show me the way to the slaughterhouse. *Moooooo!*

I want to attack your potential liberalism with truth and realism that will send you reeling, but at the same time interjecting enough fairness and humor that you can pick yourself up, dust off the ashes, and view the world with a clearer mind. Call it a form of tough love. Conservatives know what that means. You liberals are about to find out. Keep reading.

I'd like to think that everyone will enjoy reading *Liberals Don't Flush*. That won't happen. Only Conservatives will most likely reach the last page in good spirits. Lord knows it's so easy to point at the left and laugh sometimes, but I'd ask you to refrain from that impulse just as you should resist directing mirth toward a drug addict.

A liberal is very similar to a drug addict. Both are where they are because of poor choices they made. Other similarities might be failure to thrive, unhappy childhoods, self pity, self loathing, the need to escape reality, pathological lying, the search for a quick fix, succumbing to peer pressure, or about 500 other things. The simplest and most direct similarity is probably plain old human immaturity.

My goal isn't to transform you from a drooling liberal to a frothing-at-the-mouth Conservative between the first and last pages of this book. I'd like to think I had that kind of influential power in the process of saving young brains. For liberals to alter their stances with the blowing of the wind is quite common, but growing up is a difficult process and leaving behind your liberalism must be viewed in the same light.

Who am I that I should ask you to lend me your left ear? I was born in 1965 and grew up in middle class America. Atlanta, Georgia, to be exact. My father worked in the airline industry and my mother was a homemaker. I have two sisters, both younger than I by four and six years. My parents moved us to Marietta when I was ten as a measure of escaping the animalistic society of Atlanta. I attended public schools and somehow still managed to learn to read and write.

I worked for a builder, electrician, grocery store, and plumber at various times between the ages of eleven and twenty. I went to work part-time in the supply and evidence divisions of a law enforcement agency at the age of twenty-one as a means to pay for college. The intention was to obtain a degree in commercial art and then work in the field of graphic design. I instead became absorbed by the field of law enforcement. You can't work around it and not be.

My artistic skills helped me land a job as a crime scene technician. My duties included forensic art and CSI work before the television show later made much of the world believe we were magicians. I began studying serial killers and returned to college for another degree, this time in psychology. Working around police officers finally got to me and I did what I'd never intended to do. I became one of them.

I later applied to the FBI, where I very much wanted to work as a criminal profiler. I was single and willing to move wherever the Bureau might send me. I found out what affirmative action was when it crept behind me and took a nice big bite from my backside. My first experience with discrimination was as one of its victims.

Apparently I'd applied to the Bureau during a period in which my race and gender had higher requirements than did others. In simple terms … I was a white male. Various federal employees with whom I spoke after receiving the FBI's form letter told me off the record that I was the wrong color and gender at that time for a job as an agent, unless I could show unusually high qualifications. The form letter advised that I needed more education or experience. What they really meant was that I needed more education or experience to be considered equal to a minority or female, since both seemed to have a much easier time getting hired than I.

I decided to remain a police officer. I went home, collected my thick file of FBI paperwork and brochures, and threw it into the trash can. No regrets have ever haunted me. My current belief is that the FBI employees some of the best and some of the worst personnel in US law enforcement.

I married and now have two wonderful daughters. I write fiction novels in my spare time and try to stay abreast of the news of the world.

You should now understand that I'm as qualified as anyone to write about the disease called liberalism. Imagine your average altruistic and naïve little boy. Assume he's quiet, shy, and sensitive. Now throw into the mix that he eventually obtains BA's in commercial art and psychology. Would you guess that he'd be a liberal or Conservative adult? Most people would surely check the liberal box in that multiple choice question. They would be wrong in this instance. That little boy can still be quiet and shy, but he's no longer a little boy and most certainly shed himself of the naiveté. A liberal has most likely known only liberalism. A Conservative has experienced both realms, forsaking the former for the latter. I'm therefore not only highly qualified to write about liberals … I might qualify as an expert.

I'll interject my opinions because this is my book, but I also want you as the reader to consider your own opinions and how they might need to be changed. Everyone should always be doing that.

As a police officer I get to see some of the worst sort of bottom-feeders the country has to offer. That too could make me an expert on liberals. The jails are full of them.

Here we go. Move forth into the first chapter of *Liberals Don't Flush* and then proceed as your touchy-feely side struggles to maintain dominance. Laugh, cry, become angry or offended. Ingest the book like you would any other medicine for a crippling disease. One of the keys to overcoming liberalism is to break from the warm and fuzzy habit of operating solely off your feelings. You have to *think!* A whole person does both. You know … a Conservative. Learn to actually think and you could be flushing before you know it. So let's get started repairing the damage your liberal schools have done.

1

THE FRESHLY-HATCHED LIBERAL

There was once strong evidence that liberals were born in litters within the shaded areas of damp rocks. We now know otherwise. Modern science has proven that liberals are conceived and born in the traditional human manner. There are still some Conservative holdouts who swear upon the damp rock theory, but we found out years ago that we're all in fact hatched as liberals.

The time is 1:47 a.m. in the delivery room of any hospital. I'm patriotic, so let's say our setting is in America. The eastern United States to be more specific. The fluorescent lighting is intense because every nook and cranny must be saturated with light. The doctor's eyes are not as good as they once were, not because he's old, but because the American health care system has aged him beyond his years. Odds are that as an intelligent working man with a healthy income he despises liberals, so what he's about to do will be an exercise in irony.

Mom screams. Dad squeezes her hand. Out pops the freshly-hatched liberal into the doctor's hands. He looks at it. The enemy. Oooh, but it's so cute! This is like looking at a baby crocodile. Who can resist a little bit of goochy-goochy-goo? The doctor wonders if he should keep this thing or throw it back for a few more months. Perhaps the extra baking time might lessen its chances of being a lifelong liberal. Mom and Dad will have none of this idea, though. They insist upon taking the thing home after only nine months of development. Nine months? What else could the little creature have developed into but a liberal in such a short time period? Nothing is fully developed yet, especially the brain!

Dad and Mom take the little peanut home and begin the process of catering to its every need. They will cuddle it when it cries, feed it when it's hungry, provide it with toys and shelter, and wipe its little butt when it poops. Every aspect of this cycle will taper for Conservative parents until the cessation, usually by the time the hatchling has reached its eighteenth year. The process takes a bit longer for liberal parents. They will still be performing all these functions when the child applies for its beloved social security. Hmm. I just had a horrific thought. How many 4XL super-jumbo diapers do you suppose Ted Kennedy goes through in a week and who changes them? Scary.

The hatchling quickly learns to let out an ear-piercing scream to receive the things it desires. These cries will vary in intensity depending on which wants the hatching desires. The typical hatchling cry might sound something like, "Waaaaaaa-haaaaa!" A liberal who never ascends to the plateau of Conservatism by adulthood develops an array of bellows only slightly more complex than those of infancy.

One of these will be, "Where's my welfare check?" Another will be, "It's all the Republicans' fault!" These are just a couple of examples of their battle cries. Incessant and irrational bellowing in adulthood is a trait of the garden variety liberal. During their infancy we give them a pass and refer to them as colicky.

Home goes the little package with its parents. The freshly-hatched liberal of the twenty-first century currently has one chance in three of escaping its left-wing plight. You liberals would normally be delighted to hear someone painfully mention the low odds of survival for baby sea turtles scampering across the beach from nest to surf. You will not like this analogy, though. The freshly-hatched liberal will not be snatched by predators on the beach, but its odds of someday reaching Conservatism may not be much different.

Scenario number one is that the baby has Conservative parents. This is the one chance in three previously mentioned.

Scenario number two is that the baby goes home with liberal parents. This hatchling must somehow manage to overcome the almost insurmountable barriers of leftist training camp brainwashing if it's to ever reach its Conservative potential. The odds say no. Onward to number three.

Scenario number three is when the hatchling leaves the hospital with the mother only. This is because the father is unknown, unavailable, or both. Actually the proper term here isn't "father." He will formally be referred to as "my baby's daddy." This hatchling is doomed.

Life gets easier for the parents when the new liberal reaches the age of one year. The baby becomes less focused on self and more aware of and entertained by the world around. He will crawl about and gaze at things in a wondrous fog. Parents shouldn't worry at this point, because this is normal one-year-old behavior. Liberal parents will encourage this behavior well into the child's twenties. Conservative parents should see the behavior dissipate between years one and two. The same is true of any baby's tendency to play in its own dirty diaper. I reiterate that both situations are considered normal by members of the two respective tribes.

The potty-training phase can be different for each young liberal. Gender may also be a factor in training difficulty and duration. Males statistically encounter more potty-training barriers than do the females of the species. The cause of this phenomenon is unknown to modern science. What is known is that both liberal and Conservative parents usually have their children potty-trained by the fifth year. The significant difference will be that Conservatives will be able to clean themselves at a much earlier age than lifelong liberals, who will quite possibly need their butts wiped for them throughout their lives.

Young liberals will begin to play with their own genitalia during those tender years. Parents, do not panic! For little kids to explore themselves is perfectly normal. They will also compare themselves to one another as they seek to satisfy their curiosities. This too is normal. Just be aware that this ritual will typically result in the first signs of liberal jealousy of Conservative traits.

The five-year-old liberal is cute as a button. His parents will shed a few tears on that life-altering first day of school. Liberal parents cry because they're saddened to see their little lib growing up. Conservative parents cry for the same reason, but also because of the additional burden of knowing that their child has just entered *little league liberalism* by traversing the doorway into a government school. Almost all government schools are LLL certified. Parents who can afford to send their child to a private school need not worry about LLL agendas in most cases. Those rare parents who choose to home-school are sure to mold their children into whichever of the two denominations they represent.

Denominational tendencies will begin to show themselves during the elementary school years. An unnamed elementary school liberal first coined the phrase "my dog ate my homework." Note that the phrase was non-creative, self-excusing, and a falsehood. This trio of characteristics is commonly called the liberal triad. The triad will remain a hallmark of liberal behavior throughout the individual's life lest he be bathed in the healing waters of Conservatism. The primary place that we can begin to see elementary school Conservatives break from the pack will be on the playground.

Footraces are common playground engagements. A child beginning to sprout Conservative wings will be the one to suggest the race. Boys will race boys. Girls will race girls. Some inter-gender competition may also occur, but without rancor. Children who remain locked into their natural born liberalism will make claims of *unfairness* or *cheating* when they lose. Not to worry. They have a lot of developing to do and such behavior is expected. The time to worry comes if they're still engaging in such behavior by their seventeenth year (or 193 months, for you liberal parents). These footraces will more often occur upon the grounds of private schools. Competition will be referred to as "the C-word" by many government school teachers and strongly discouraged if not altogether forbidden.

Another long-time playground practice has been playing on monkey bars. You can spot modern budding Conservatives by listening closely to monkey bar interaction, because they continue to call the equipment "monkey bars." Little libs will be discouraged from using such terminology in the twenty-first century by their mentors. Liberals must consider the possibility that people could be offended by having their children playing on something called "monkey bars," the potential implication being that the children have something in common with monkeys. Not to be ignored would also be the possibility of offending monkeys.

The assumption must be made that monkeys could be offended by the terminology, since we cannot yet ask them. Recent studies have been conducted in California and New England states, where the gap between man and ape is rapidly closing. Those studies have thus far supported the concept that monkeys are indeed offended by the phrase "monkey bars."

Just finding a set of monkey bars amongst the plastics of today's playgrounds may be somewhat difficult, but older schools and parks may contain them. Find such a place and observe the behavior of children at play. Children with Conservative wiring can be overheard saying something like, "Let's swing on the monkey bars!" Liberal pups will refer to them exactly as at least one past US President insisted that his interns refer to his genitalia: *non-linear play-thingies.*

Sharing is an interesting phenomenon at this period in the lives of children. Sharing is like so many other things that must be experienced in moderation. Too little and we never taste the true joy of the act. Too much and others may come to take advantage of us. Watching children engage in the act of sharing warms the heart. They may share food, let slower children win an occasional footrace, or yield space on the antiquated monkey bar play-thingie.

The habit of sharing isn't distinctive to the denominational boundaries of liberals and Conservatives until the human being reaches an age of expected self-sufficiency. The two creatures then become bitterly distinct. Conservatives will still practice moderation, but the demands of the liberals will become intense. They will in fact come to expect the Conservatives to provide for their very survival and the once cordial childhood interaction will turn bitter. Strange creatures, these human beings.

The last playground behavior that will be noted is similar to sharing in that liberals will eventually misdirect their behavior and engage without substance. Those who reach some level of Conservatism will sublimate this behavior into more honorable formats, once again out-maturing the liberals. The act of which I speak here is the throwing of sticks and rocks.

Liberals aren't yet dangerous during these early years. Skewed thinking is to be expected. There are no hard lines between Conservatives and liberals at the freshly-hatched stage of life. The lines are instead both delicate and dynamic. The few who display strong Conservative tendencies early are probably natural leaders. They will never regress from those tendencies. That's the good news for young Conservatives.

The good news for liberals is that it's never too late to begin earning your Conservative stripes. Allow concepts such as responsibility, accountability, and common sense to pass through the blood-brain barrier. I don't mean to oversimplify your chances. The pathway to Conservatism usually begins with the parents giving their hatchling loving nudges from the branches of life so he or she may learn to fly.

You liberals ... yikes! You will have to walk yourselves to the ends of the various branches and jump! Fat chance, unfortunately. A couple of you might actually survive, but most will drop into your respective soup lines and join the ranks of the undead. The most you can hope for might be a senate seat ... perhaps in Massachusetts. Any questions?

2

THE CRITICAL YEARS

The concept and title of *Liberals Don't Flush* refers to the process of making a big mess of things and leaving the dirty work to someone else. The primary area in which this applies to liberals falling short is rearing children.

Raising children is without a doubt the toughest job in the world and is therefore the main area in which liberals shirk their duties. They've never been much for tough work no matter what the topic: raising children, serving honorably in the military, earning honest wages, etcetera. Liberals will ironically work their hardest at trying to avoid work. At this one task they will forever excel.

Let us refer to the critical years as those relevant to the high school years for the purpose of this chapter. These years are in fact critical because many new waters will be tested. Opinions form and reform. The brain is like a living piece of clay from birth, struggling amongst the forces within and from the outside world, trying to molt its liberal layers to eventually solidify into glorious Conservatism. These critical years represent the half to three-quarter mark of this development.

Little kids think their parents know everything. Any question a small child asks can be answered by a parent in a way that will satisfy the child. These questions will become more elaborate over time and a crucial milestone will occur at some point during adolescence. A teenager will ask questions that cannot be answered satisfactorily and some perhaps not at all, and the youth will come to the realization that his parents in fact don't know everything.

Conservative parents will readily admit this to their sons and daughters. There will be no animosity from adolescent Conservatives regarding this realization. Their confidence will actually benefit from the discovery. Conservative parents with a teen still floating within the mist of liberal thought can use this time as a way to help him or her take another step up the ladder of Conservatism.

Liberal parents cannot accept the idea that they don't know everything, so their route will be to back up and change their responses to tough questions from their teens. They will twist truths until something seems to fit closely enough to be acceptable. Their uncanny ability to spin these confusing webs explains why many of these folks have such promising careers as reporters, politicians, and lawyers. Doesn't do much for their poor children, though.

Children lie. They can be brutally honest, but they also lie. Everybody with kids knows that.

"Did you poop?" you may ask your little two-year-old cutie.

The response might be "no" even though her swollen pants smell like low tide at a water treatment facility.

Small children sometimes fabricate stories. That's to be expected within the hatchling years. Dishonesty becomes less tolerable as the child leaves its hatchling years behind. A lying adolescent is another matter altogether ... unless the parents fully intend to keep him in his fog of liberalism forever. Lying is within that context considered to be one of the basic arts of a liberal in training.

Honesty is an important rung of the ladder of Conservatism. The rung isn't far above the unstable ground of liberal muck, but it's utterly amazing how many people never reach even that far due to lack of willpower or integrity. The overwhelming majority of adolescents fully understand the behavior of lying. They know it's wrong, but lying has for a liberal upstart always been a vehicle of accountability avoidance.

Again, the two-year-old liberal pup might claim his diaper is empty despite his staggering against the extra weight. A fully grown lib will say such things as "I didn't inhale." The pup is considered a *cutie*. The adult is what may commonly be referred to as a *flaming left-winger*. Both versions of liberal have one thing in common despite obvious differences in size and chronological age. They're both full of crap.

A child of the later freshly-hatched years or early critical years will have an eye-opening realization one afternoon. He'll be a shut-in for the day for telling yet another lie to his parents. The child of Conservatives will be under orders to sit and think about what he's done. A child of some borderline liberals might also briefly find himself in his room for the same infraction, but he'll be allowed to surf the Web or play with his Xbox 360 and PlayStation system while he awaits the fulfillment of his sentence.

A child will make his first great leap toward Conservatism at the moment he figuratively hears a voice inside his head tell him, *you need to stop telling lies. You're not good at it. You always get caught and trying to pass off lies as truths is a tremendous burden on the mind.* This child just acknowledged an important part of his being that will eventually wither into nonexistence in the common liberal. A conscience.

An adolescent that gets himself into trouble will be dealt with in two very unique manners by parents from the two denominational schools of thought. Let's use the old baseball breaks a window scenario. Let's adopt as our model a thirteen-year-old male who tosses a baseball into the air and hits it toward a house with a bat. The ball breaks a window and goes into the house. The boy gets scared and runs home.

The homeowner calls the boy's parents. Our first example involves Conservative parents. They will ask the boy what happened. He will be punished if he lies and the cost of the window will be withdrawn from his allowance, if he receives one. Nothing much will happen if he tells the truth. He won't be punished severely if at all, but must still pay for the window for running from the scene. The next time something like this occurs … he won't run.

Now take the same young videogame jockey and toss liberal parents into the mix. You'll hear the phrase "boys will be boys" used several times as the parents defend their son. The defense will become more intense until the parents have become the boy's dream team defense attorneys. You know, the kind that will attempt to defeat every piece of overwhelming evidence that comes their way. The homeowner will grow angry and decide that calling the police will be the only chance she has not only at restitution, but at a lesson of accountability for the youthful slugger.

"How can you be sure my son broke the window?" the flaming liberal parent will ask the officer.

"The homeowner heard her window break and found this baseball in her living room."

"So?"

"The homeowner saw your son running away. No one was with him and he carried a baseball bat."

"So?"

"The ball has his name on it."

"My son can't be the only boy in the world named Cletus Geronimo Moldlobe. Is the alleged incident in question on videotape?"

"No, of course not."

"Then it didn't really happen, officer. Any further questions can be directed to my attorney."

"All right. What's your attorney's name?"

"I don't have to answer that on the grounds that it calls for speculation ... or something."

So goes the process of a liberal solidifying unaccountability and lack of integrity into Liberal, Jr. These adolescents don't have a prayer of ever reaching even the first rung up the ladder of Conservatism. They're as perfectly content to swim in the muck of liberalism as were their mothers and their mothers' babys' daddies.

Youthful idealism is a wonderful thing. You can become a fully-developed Conservative adult and still retain some worthwhile pieces of childhood. The happiest people in fact do. The youthful thoughts and behaviors require guidance, though. With no guidance the ingredients become the makings of runaway liberal thought, from which there is no chance of recovery. Guidance and accountability are the two primary things that every adolescent will need. Otherwise he'll still be in need of them when he's the President of the United States.

There are a lot of firsts to be faced by a high school kid. The first date. The first kiss. Possibly a first job ... known as the "J-word" by welfare recipients. More important than any of these will be that old ugly "C-word" again. That's right ... *competition*. You liberals cover your ears. You Conservatives shout it aloud. *Competition!*

There's a lot of competition in high school. Competition for social positioning. Competition on the sports fields. Artistic competition. Academic competition. What I propose is that there's a more intense brand of competition out there and a high school kid may well struggle with it for the first time in his or her young life. I'm talking about competition with self.

Most children will experience the realization at some point between the first and twelfth grades that they can actually study, learn, and do well in school if they apply themselves. This wonderful realization can even occur for those of us who attend government schools. I know, because mine occurred in the eleventh grade. Competition with self simply refers to the process of doing the best you can at the tasks you undertake. You'll find that the more steps taken up the ladder of Conservatism, the less willing you'll be to settle for less than your best. Achievement is quite addictive to the budding Conservative and he begins working toward his Master Flusher badge.

The child who is on the pathway of succumbing to liberalism will have begun the process of shunning competition, including the self type. A budding liberal will find solace in the fact that his government school has the same philosophy regarding competition. Achievement is okay as long as all kids are constantly kept on a level playing field.

Achievement in liberal structure means that everyone gets herded toward the average of everything in life. Young liberals who find themselves falling behind academically need not worry in government schools. The system is designed to afford them whatever academic points they require to qualify for academic mediocrity. Kids who engage in the more popular athletic sports will also be taken care of academically. This will continue not only throughout grade school, but college as well.

"But why would a liberal child want to participate in athletics?" you ask. "That's competition."

Don't forget that entitlement mentality isn't limited to the poor or non-athletic. Right, Terrell Owens? Right, O.J? Don't make the elementary mistake of believing that a capable body translates to a capable mind anymore than the reverse would be true.

I've already mentioned the fact that youthful non-flushers aren't held accountable for their actions by their best friends and personal defense lawyers who call themselves "parents." The lack of behavioral structure and accountability leads to behavioral problems that traverse all aspects of a child's life. Parents who spare not only the rod but all other measures of discipline need not fear. Modern science has sent a trench-coated fiend to an alleyway near you and he's equipped with just what you want … a diagnosis of ADHD and a fix of Ritalin.

"Psst. Hey, kid. C'mere."

Once the fiend throws open that trench coat the child has a substitute and false set of parents … Mr. ADHD and Mrs. Ritalin. They provide a façade of control. Also in the fiend's trench coat can be found steroids if an athletic boost is sought, heroin or marijuana for a desired altered state, and crack or methamphetamine if your teen is feeling a little run-down. If you're going to remain a liberal, then you've got to be prepared to go all the way.

Nothing is cemented during the critical years of adolescence. Change occurs almost daily, to which the parents of many teens can attest. Liberalism is still the predominant denomination of human life throughout adolescence. Only ten percent of the freshly-hatched herd displays any concept of Conservatism. This expectation only rises to twenty percent by the latter months of high school adolescence.

These figures are higher for children attending private schools, but who can afford that? Certainly not the majority. We therefore rely on our amazingly inefficient government to teach our children. Is it any wonder that only twenty percent of new adults think with predominantly Conservative thought circuits?

Conservatives would say that's one in five that has been rescued from the pit. Liberals would say that's one in five that the system has lost to the enemy.

"Don't give up at this point," say the liberals. "There's still college."

3

LIBERAL STATE UNIVERSITY

The theme of American grade schools could be "Education … or lack thereof." The issue of concern with American colleges isn't whether or not education is actually taking place. They're most definitely educating. The question is what are they teaching?

A popular trend in modern times has become rewriting history. People take from history those pieces that support their personal agendas. Everything else they either eliminate or twist into something more favorable to their views. This activity has been solely practiced by the left. One of the darlings of the left is Iranian President Mahmoud Ahmadinejad, who amongst his other rants of insanity has declared that the Holocaust never occurred. The whole thing was just a big farce. If you actually believe that he's correct, then close this book right now and hand it to someone who actually has a functioning brain. May I also suggest that your next step should be to buy a one-way ticket to Iran? Vacancies are also available in France.

You're eighteen years old and just stepped through the doorway to your first college class. The odds are higher than ever that you're going to be instructed by a thirty-five-year-old diaper-wearing liberal who will take opportunities to expound on his or her personal views. You're right at home if your intention is to remain a lefty yourself, but what do you do if you want something better for yourself and that rapidly solidifying mass between your ears? Worse yet, what if like so many college students you don't really know what you want to do or what you really think about this world?

You're definitely endangered by having just walked into one of the most concentrated liberal cell pockets scattered across this nation … an American university campus. Liberalism is the easy road. Conservatism is the tougher row to hoe, but far more productive in the long run. You have only a few years to decide what you want for yourself and the time goes quickly. So which do you think you'll select: the ease of the idealistic route or the realism and responsibility of the Conservative lifestyle? You used to be a cute little runny-nosed liberal like everyone else, but now the clock is ticking. You're an adult.

Sean Hannity has done a wonderful job of exposing the university system as a network of liberalism far more dangerous to our future than terrorist cells. We've always known of what terrorists are capable. We're finally learning of the cancerous evil that lurks within American colleges and universities. Liberalism.

Mr. Hannity aired some tapes that students had recorded in their classes of instructors speaking in the forked tongues of liberalism. The recordings were both enlightening and terrifying to hear. Rumors were that at least two of these professors' heads spun completely around as they ranted and that a vile green liquid was spewed forth, but these reported sightings haven't been substantiated. No visual effects were necessary. The sounds of their anti-Americanism, hatred for the US Military, and attempts to undermine President Bush were quite enough.

The segments were sickening to listen to if you have even one Conservative bone in your body. The true definition of higher learning should be that which can be learned from the likes of Sean Hannity, Michael Savage, Neal Boortz, Ann Coulter, Herman Cain, and Rush Limbaugh, as opposed to these dirty-diapered liberal college professors who don't flush.

A college education isn't what it used to be. The feeling in the air is that degrees are issued at the drop of a hat. Talk to business owners about the people they employ. Ask them if they notice differences between their college-educated employees and those without college. You might be surprised to find that the business owner's most valued employees had no college at all. Amongst those with college degrees it might also be discovered that the least coveted workers came to the business via the more prestigious schools. Can you feel that, Ted? Truth stings, doesn't it?

The liberal invasion of the American university system has reached an all-time high. The results: an all-time low work ethic, an all-time high sense of entitlement, clouded and bastardized thought processes, and an expectation that everyone should live within the leftist cotton candy world of idealism. Leftist professors push socialism like drug dealers.

A Conservative student who voices his views may very well be treated as an outcast. The results may even be seen in the student's grades if they cross these liberal professors in disagreement over opinions. Not much can be manipulated with multiple choice tests, but beware the professors' treatments of more subjective efforts such as narrative answers, lab reports, or semester projects.

How deeply does the problem run? To the bone! Much of the country was shocked to learn that Yale University had not only admitted but aggressively recruited Sayed Rahmatullah Hashemi as a student. Who is he? He's formerly of the noxious Taliban! Other so-called elite schools have committed similar atrocities. Let that sink in for a moment. Hashemi was welcomed with open arms into Yale University.[1] Is that shocking? The idea shouldn't be shocking at all when you consider the state of mind across our university system. Liberals are terrorist sympathizers, so why should we be surprised to find a terrorist attending Yale? Maybe Hashemi can eventually be a Yale professor. I'm sure there will be a job waiting for him somewhere when the time comes.

Lines are being drawn in the sand in the United States. The liberal serpents will keep pushing their agendas and the nature of Conservatives is to fight back when attacked. The vision of the future isn't a pretty one. I look at history and our current state of affairs and can't help but see impending turmoil within our own country.

I've drawn some lines of my own in recent years. Issues that used to be neutral for me rapidly became polarized. Other Conservatives will know that feeling and what I'm talking about. We refuse to bend to the leftist agendas. This is war in more than one way. War is underway in the Middle East with guns and bombs, but there's another war building right here on our own soil called the war of thought. Our very own way of life in America is at stake and Conservatives will not bend to left-wing terrorist apologists. Mr. Hashemi shouldn't be attending Yale University. He probably shouldn't even be breathing. He should be tried as an American combatant and executed if guilty. If you're not willing to accept the responsibility of remaining loyal to our country, then you're on the other side of the line in the sand. Yale University … you are the enemy.

Now pick up your lower jaw from the floor and understand that I'm not promoting the idea that Conservatives should ignore their human feelings. Only a liberal would've drawn that conclusion from my comments. To the contrary. We as human beings can never lose touch with our emotions and feelings. They're one of the few things that separate us from being monsters, such as the ones who compose nests of murderers like the Taliban and al-Qaeda. We must hold fast to a strong conscience, because only by keeping ourselves in check should we expect to be afforded any power or control by our fellow countrymen.

So how do you as the eighteen-year-old fence rider between the Conservatives on the right and liberals on the left know which way to turn? Don't think you can keep riding that fence. Try that and someone from one side or the other is bound to knock you off sooner or later. An issue will arise and you'll be forced to choose. College professors tend to demand decisiveness, so be prepared or you're going to fall off the left side of that fence into a pile of muck in which you don't wish to be.

Liberalism in America can be summed into one word. *Avoidance.* Young people are subjected to the liberal mindset and trained for *avoidance* in American colleges. Avoidance of reality. Avoidance of responsibility. Avoidance of any sense of duty. Avoidance of loyalty. Avoidance of accountability. And the biggest one … avoidance of truth.

What is avoidance of reality? Most high school students and a large number of college students walk around with their heads in the clouds anyway. Many college professors feel it's their job to keep you there. The touchy-feely-warm-and-fuzzy approach to life can be humorous in the movies, but it's not funny in real life. A liberal is weak and knows so, but tries to present a front of decisiveness and security. He has neither and the front is thin. Here's an example of reality avoidance:

Picture one of our garden variety college educated lefties standing outside a polar bear exhibit. Let's say she's wearing a Liberal State University shirt, has a tongue stud and nose ring, and totes a personal CD player. She has several CD's in her backpack: Madonna, Sheryl Crow, Barbra Streisand, REM, but right now she's listening to rap. Take your pick which "artist." The backpack is of non-animal origin, because leather is such a barbaric material. Stuffed in there amongst the CD's and bologna & cheese is yesterday's *New York Times*. She didn't read the paper, but it will look good displayed beside her on the park bench later as she eats her sandwich.

She sees the DANGER sign on the polar bear exhibit and immediately rejects it. Every good liberal must learn to ignore rules and authority. The DANGER sign doesn't apply to her. The sign was put there by a Conservative after all. Only a Conservative could've been so cruel as to cage a polar bear in the first place. The evil Conservative surely sees the bear as a predator. A monster. She sees the bear for what it really is … a big cuddly ball of white fur that wouldn't harm her if she just climbed right into the pit with him. Over the wall she goes. The bear eats the liberal, the backpack, and all other contents. He spits out the Streisand CD.

Avoidance of responsibility refers to the countless ways that liberals almost always take the easy roads of life. The only thing they seem determined to work at is making sure that someone else feels obligated to take care of them. They're in love with words like socialism and welfare. Liberals with power have simply been elevated to their positions by the leeches of the left to be their spokesmen and spokeswomen. They have no goals beyond breathing the air and drawing paychecks … as long as they don't have to actually work.

There are contrasts between a Conservative President and a liberal one on the concept of responsibility. A Conservative President tends to try to gather us together outside the polar bear pit and he says, "Enjoy the beauty of the view, but acknowledge the DANGER sign."

A liberal president tends to say, "Screw the sign. Everybody into the pit who wants to go. Those who choose not to enter should analyze what it is that we could've possibly done to piss off this bear."

Avoidance of duty and loyalty are favorites of our modern university system. People tend to think of the military when words like duty and loyalty are mentioned. I think of Douglas MacArthur. One thing you absolutely must accomplish if you've decided to be a diaper-wearing liberal is an intense hatred of the US Military forces. That's on page one of the liberal bible. Expect to have history taught to you with a contemporary twist. Some professors may not be able to twist the curriculum enough, so there's always the option of making stuff up. Many college professors write books that are used in college classrooms. Scary.

A sense of duty and loyalty to our country should be a given. Every American should consider it an honor to be a part of this country and that includes legal immigrants. Men and women have battled to make this a place of freedom, giving up their lives and those of their loved ones so that we could inherit a consistently free and strong United States of America.

I consider it an unforgivable insult that some panty-waste liberal college professor should attempt to undermine the sacrifices of those who came before us, especially when the only things for which he ever had to fight were to beat his possession charges and to gain a spot on the school newspaper staff.

Avoidance of duty and loyalty extends to all facets of liberal life, not just their views of the American Military. Liberals will only remain rigidly loyal and show any sense of duty to their backing of radically leftist organizations. The Democratic Party has become one of these in recent years.

Other concepts liberals wholeheartedly support are socialism, communism, anti-Americanism, unrealistic feel-good environmentalism, fanning flames of racism, and of course the homosexual agenda. Simply put, an American has a duty to be loyal to this country based solely upon our history.

Avoidance of accountability is the skeletal system of liberalism. There is no actual Avoidance of Accountability 101 college course of which I know, but liberal college graduates so often seem to be experts on the topic. Their expertise becomes more ingrained and polished as time passes. Lucrative occupations that utilize AOA skills are readily available for those wishing to become criminal defense lawyers, white collar criminals, politicians, members of the media, college professors, rock stars, actors, illegal aliens, or terrorists.

Accountability avoidance manifests itself in a variety of ways. One is the popular act of screaming "racism" when you get caught doing something wrong or when you don't get your way. Another is to spontaneously regurgitate a list of excuses as long as the Koran in an effort to cover wrongdoing. These folks find it exceedingly difficult to say "my bad" or "I'm sorry" after committing life's simplest mistakes. Let the finger-pointing begin. Everything will always be someone else's fault.

Two liberals walk into an elevator. The formerly fresh air soon begins to smell of the distinctive scent of methane. They look at one another and simultaneously declare, "It wasn't me!"

That little parable perfectly illustrates the failure of accountability that composes the core of liberal life. By the way ... both liberals in the elevator were guilty, just in case you were wondering.

The skeleton of liberalism is avoidance of accountability, so the muscular system has to be avoidance of truth. Avoidance of truth is the driving force of the left not only in most American colleges, but dominates liberal life from the freshly-hatched stage to death. Let's call AOT what it really is. Lying.

Liberals don't have a monopoly on lying. We're all capable given the wrong circumstances, like when we find ourselves in trouble and upon a hot-seat. An interesting exhibition can usually be found in watching as a liberal tries to debate an orally competent Conservative. The liberal will resort to blatant falsehoods the more the Conservative turns up the heat with truth. A couple of the Masters at turning up that heat are Sean Hannity and Ann Coulter, for those interested in witnessing professional verbal battles. For you guys out there who have never seen Ann Coulter ... she's worth watching even when the TV is muted. You girls may feel similarly about Hannity, but I'm afraid I'm not qualified to make that assumption.

Dr. Michael Savage regularly and appropriately diagnoses liberalism as a mental disorder. Liberal State University is full of these demented people, both within the student body and faculty. A frothing-at-the-mouth liberal college professor may actually believe the platforms of the left to be true and accurate. He or she qualifies as demented on that basis alone. Listen to them talk, then flip through the *Diagnostic and Statistical Manual of Mental Disorders* and label them appropriately. If ADHD can have a listing within the *DSM*, then liberalism deserves its own chapter.

I reiterate that children can be brutally honest sometimes, but they can also say things that aren't true. The tendency to tell lies must be overcome through maturity and accountability. The fact that we're all born as liberals has already been discussed, as has the realization that the affliction can be overcome. The process isn't as easy as obtaining a senate seat or getting elected as President, so is it any wonder that liberal college professors are a dime a dozen? I frankly wouldn't pay a dime for the majority of the dishonest lot.

A liberal college professor is like a serial killer. He's reached the pinnacle of his career, but ironically becomes a more destructive force the harder he works. He knows what he does is wrong. He secretly wishes that someone would just put him out of his misery, but he just can't stop his downward spiral.

Conservatism is a tough and rewarding road. Liberalism is an easy road, shrouded in the mist of concepts and theories. The Liberal State University library is filled with volumes of information on those self-serving concepts and theories, but you probably won't find a book by a Conservative. The reason is because preaching leftist theory allows lying to occur under the cloak of philosophy. Do you think a Conservative or a liberal is more likely to become a private business owner, and which do you think is more likely to become a philosopher? I don't recall seeing any philosophy offices within the commercial districts I've been through. That's because the only places they can find jobs are as college professors or politicians.

Living the lies of liberalism is easy in college. Some of the students will find their niches there and decide to become college professors. Being a liberal within America's productive work force isn't so easy. A college graduate with his head in the mist of liberalism gets a rude awakening when he actually has to go to work, pay taxes, and stop completely relying on assistance from mommy and daddy.

A college graduate sits upon the fence between Conservatism and liberalism, but he's still probably facing to the left. He's also scowling, since that fence is topped with barbed wire. Our liberal graduate may fall to the left, into the muck that's always provided his childhood comfort zone. Free thought. Free action. Lack of responsibility and accountability. All very appealing to the pleasure-seeking parts of the brain. His other choice is to decide to finally grow up and he turns his head to the right to see what's over there. There's no turning back once he sees the greener grass of Conservatism. The creatures of the left gnash their teeth at him as he steps into the opposing field. Another one saved from the liar's lair to the kingdom of what's *right*.

Extreme liberal thoughts are like breast implants for the mind. The American university system is the hack installing them. Liberalism and breast implants. Only a couple of good things can result from either and the rest is all bad.

4

LEFT BRAIN-RIGHT BRAIN

This is one of the very few areas in which the liberals are right. Quite possibly the only one. Everybody knows at least in general terms that the right hemisphere of the brain is documented as the half associated with creative expression. The left side processes logic, language, etcetera. Let's keep this simple. The left-brainer is the pragmatist. The right-brainer is the dreamer.

A left-brained person would most likely make a good orator, accountant, business person, or card player. Examine the work of Albert Einstein for amazing examples of what the left hemisphere of the brain is capable of producing.

A right-brained person has a much higher likelihood of being suited to artistic creativity. The right-brainer may write stories, play music, act, paint, or design clothing. Can you imagine Mozart teaching an economics course? I can't either, but I bet the man could've written an opera about teaching economics that would've been just lovely.

Some people are geared much more to one brain hemisphere than the other, but I'm not implying that liberals have the creative market cornered and Conservatives the logic market. Human beings are far more complex than that. The computer that we have between our ears doesn't function on just one lobe at a time. The visual part of the brain is at the rear. You may see a flash of white light if you get struck hard enough near the back of the skull. You liberals feel free to practice that on one another anytime.

We don't just see something and not experience thoughts or emotions in conjunction with the visual experience, though. I don't look at a picture of Faith Hill and just *see* the image. I promise that neurons are firing across the entire map of my brain. I've tested this many times.

Consider the work of an architect. He must be able to utilize some degree of artistic visualization and have good graphic illustration skills, but for his creation to come to life he must also know a little something about structural engineering and mathematics.

An inventor may conceptualize an idea for a new product, draw the product, and then build it. Both hemispheres are at work. Men are said to be more capable than women at mapping skills. You can test this for yourself. Just ask a woman for directions or to indicate which direction is north. Lots of luck. Men are more likely to be able to visualize a Rubik's Cube, rotate it within the mind, and still be able to tell in which positions the colors are located. Women are said to have a thicker corpus callosum than men, which is the biological bridge connecting the two hemispheres of the brain. From that we can draw the conclusion that women can more efficiently use the two hemispheres of the brain simultaneously. We may therefore draw the inference that the mighty corpus callosum is opposed to any interaction between logic and financial discipline.

The point is that there are a lot of factors at play within the human mind and it's for that reason that we must generalize our left brain-right brain discussion. The greatest artist or musician in the world could very well be a Conservative. The world's greatest scientist could be a flaming lib. I use myself as a glowing example of the way these factors interact. I write fiction. I draw. I paint ... sort of. I own a guitar, bass, synthesizer, violin, mandolin, and saxophone. I also possess the occasional ability to think and act with logic and reason, and consider myself a far right Conservative. Any artistic endeavor I undertake just might be a way of blowing off steam due to anger induced by the left. I guess you could call a combined effort of the hemispheres *creative logic*. Creative logic is used by the more successful police officers. A cop can go a long way in his duties just using logic, but throw creative drive into the mix and you will witness some unique and effective police work.

Now back to the generalization that right-brainers are dreamers and probably compose the majority of all liberals. Why should we have to listen to the illogical rants of the entertainment industry, especially with any sense of seriousness? What makes actors and musicians believe that the masses should seriously consider the social and political opinions of people who live in fantasy land? What makes the likes of Madonna, Harry Bellafonte, and Alec Baldwin believe that their views of the world should be heard? The liberal-biased news media gives such people a platform from which to speak and that will continue. After all, the news media is largely composed of actors and writers who weren't good enough to make the big time. I don't believe the reason liberal entertainers should be heard is because everyone should have a voice. I think they should be heard because their warm and fuzzy stupidity serves the right by exposing liberals for the mess-makers they are. Hey Alec, Harry needs his diaper changed again. I'll change Madonna.

I boycott left-wing entertainers more than I used to. My favorite rock band of over twenty years dropped from my radar screen because the lead singer spouted his leftist viewpoints once too often. I thought *The Hunt for Red October* and *The Edge* were terrific movies, but I can no longer look upon Alec Baldwin without hearing his insane pissing and moaning.

Paul Newman's salad dressing used to be my favorite even though his acting never did much for me. I don't buy the dressing anymore since seeing his name more than once amongst a list of celebrities who support cop killer Mumia Abu-Jamal.

I really liked *Collateral* when I saw it the first five times on DVD, despite Tom Cruise. I'm not real sure what Tom Cruise is, though. I'm not convinced that anyone does, including Tom Cruise. Let's just call him a liberal. No Conservative acts like that and "nut job" isn't an official party choice.

Two of my favorite movies of all time are *Jaws* and *Close Encounters of the Third Kind*, certainly not because of Richard Dreyfuss, but both happen to contain his work. Dreyfuss attempted to destroy these favorites of mine in early 2006 by spouting Bush-bashing bull. Thanks, Rick.

You members of the entertainment industry, listen up! Do what you were backed to do by the fans who elevated you to wherever you are. Act in movies, play music, write poetry, paint portraits, or just act a fool, but beyond that shut the hell up and leave the analysis of social situations and politics to those who still have a zip code somewhere near reality!

Natalie Maines! Alec Baldwin! Chevy Chase! Danny Glover! Tim Robbins! Susan Sarandon! Martin Sheen! Cameron Diaz! You and your kind, hear me now. You speak for a cult of mindless rabble, not for the United States of America!

#@*%$!!! Now I feel like *I* need to paint a portrait. Where's my red paint and meat cleaver?

There either seems to be a very short list of Hollywood Conservatives or else most of them keep quiet for fear of upsetting the socialistic apple cart that dominates their livelihood. Isn't it ironic that one of the best Presidents the United States has ever seen came from their ranks? I was first eligible to vote in the 1984 election and it was an honor to punch a hole next to the name Ronald Reagan. The '80s represent our last great era for more than just music. Do you think perhaps that one of our future great Presidents is currently starring in action flicks? Unlikely, but maybe. Singing country music? Possibly. A rock star? Uh ... not.

Can anyone think of just one movie that was enjoyed by the masses and yet had a traditional message of morality that Conservatives can be proud of? I can. *A*

Charlie Brown Christmas was released in 1965, never ages, and you can watch it in July when the temperature is pushing 100. Thank you and God bless you, Charles Shulz.

I understand the occasional pleasure of disconnecting responsible thought processes and letting the brain go to sleep while the eyes are still open. This is like a brief vacation for the mind. Watch a movie, listen to music, draw or paint, go fishing, or lie in the grass and watch the clouds float by. Just make sure you switch your brain on again before doing something as critical as walking into an election booth. Otherwise we get embarrassments such as the likes of Jimmy Carter and Bill Clinton. Both nurtured situations through their weaknesses that necessitated military conflicts later. They made huge messes and left the flushing to Conservative successors. Their predecessors should've left them signs at the White House reading, *Please Clean Up After Yourselves! Your Mother Doesn't Work Here!* Carter and Clinton. Now there's a couple of guys to be proud of.

Serpents like Adolph Hitler, Osama bin Laden, Saddam Hussein, and Mahmoud Ahmadinejad will always insure that war is waged. Spineless liberals like Jimmy Carter and Bill Clinton insure through their policies and beliefs that the campaigns will be as long and bloody as possible.

I'd give the following advice to people heading to the polls for any election. If you haven't investigated a particular race or aren't sure about it ... don't vote on that issue! You could do more harm than good. An election is a serious matter that affects us all and shouldn't be taken lightly; it's not a guessing game. Be more intelligent than the cattle most of your elected officials believe you to be. Rake the prejudicial chips from your shoulders and leave them at home. A photo ID will be required, but you won't need your race cards.

In other words ... use your brains. Both hemispheres if possible. Calling all liberals. This is your chance to show us your left side.

5

THE INJUSTICE SYSTEM

I always thought when I was a kid that the American "justice system" was actually just. Then I got a firsthand look at its incompetence and prejudice when I was eighteen. Bear with me as I detail this extended story.

My best friend and I were seated in his pickup truck in a parking lot where teens from our high school used to cruise. We weren't there to cause problems. Various people had stopped to talk to us and had moved on. A light-colored Toyota pickup truck containing three adults stopped in front of us perpendicularly. The right side passenger got out and approached us. The scraggly male had dark and greasy collar-length hair, a week's growth of beard stubble, and a light jacket. He looked twice our ages.

The male approached the driver's side of my friend's truck and pulled a .44 magnum revolver from a shoulder holster. He pointed the weapon at my friend and proceeded to carry on a conversation with him that made no sense to us. I could smell the odor of an alcoholic beverage on the man's breath all the way across the cab of the pickup. The suspect talked almost exclusively to my friend and I don't recall much of the conversation. I looked straight ahead. You tend to only say "yes sir" when there's a .44 in your face, and you do so with great sincerity and politeness. My friend said "yes sir" several times to whatever was being asked or ordered, but the suspect still cocked the hammer on the revolver to accent whatever insane point he'd been trying to make. I remember putting my hand on the door handle and thinking, *if I hear that gun go off ... I've got to at least try to get away.*

We were released after several minutes that seemed like an hour. We left the parking lot, but were not the types to let such things slide. We waited in the area until the Toyota pickup left the parking lot and we followed to get a tag number for the police. We got behind the Toyota truck in traffic only to find that there was no tag on it. Whoever was driving the Toyota attempted to turn around and pursue us, but my friend's truck was a '68 Ford with a 390 engine and we were able to easily escape the situation at that point.

We found a county police officer a couple of miles away in a parking lot and we made a report. The matter ended there for the time being.

Some weeks later my friend showed me a picture of the suspect who had held us at gunpoint. I was ecstatic that the nut-job had been identified. The photograph was in a yearbook of uniformed people. The name next to the suspect's picture was Allen Thomas Bailey. I looked at the cover of the yearbook and couldn't believe what my eyes were seeing. *Atlanta Police Department.*

My friend's mother was a secretary at the county police department where we had filed our report, which was how he'd obtained the APD yearbook following the identification process. I asked him how this had transpired and he told me the following:

He'd encountered a female at a local hangout a week or two prior to the incident involving the gun. The two of them had words about something, so she'd had her brother scare him by pointing out my friend's truck the night I was with him. She'd been one of the other two people in the Toyota that night.

I asked my friend how he'd been able to make the connection. He explained that he'd recently encountered the same female, and she approached and asked something like, "So how did you like my brother?"

"What do you mean?"

"My brother ... the one who scared the shit out of you at the Kmart," I imagine she smugly announced. "He's an Atlanta police officer."

"Oh, really? What's his name?"

"Allen T. Bailey."

"Thanks."

Away my friend drove with the information necessary for the county police handling his case to conduct a photographic line-up. They're going to bury this guy, I thought. He was an off-duty cop outside his jurisdiction and pulled a gun on two teenagers in a shopping center to make a point about something trivial. He's going to be toast, I thought.

I was a good kid who made decent grades and avoided trouble completely. I'd simply been pulled into this idiocy by being in the wrong place at the wrong time. I figured that we would tell our sides of the story and the defense couldn't possibly say much to counter us. After all ... we would probably be the only ones telling the truth.

We were told that the reason the APD uniform officer had looked so scraggly the night of the incident had been because he'd been on leave from his duties.

He'd apparently come home to find his wife with another man and the boyfriend had shot him.

We also found out that the fine upstanding Officer A.T. Bailey had punched a game room owner earlier the same night as our encounter with him. The game room owner would also be testifying at the trial. Terrific, I thought. We can't lose. I also remember thinking, *this guy is a police officer? What kind of trailer trash are they hiring at APD?*

By now you've probably figured out that the jury let this guy off. You would be correct. Bailey appeared in court with his hair cut, clean shaven, and yes … wearing his police uniform he so masterfully disgraced every time he wore it.

He'd hired a belly-crawling attorney from Austell to represent him. The belly-crawler was permitted to call us liars in open court. I'd always prided myself on my honesty (after I outgrew my liberal youth) and I took tremendous offense to the suggestion that I'd come to court to lie on behalf of my friend. The suspect's sister appeared in court wearing a dress that was so short the judge ordered her to place her jacket upon her lap.

Nice try, cupcake. I guess you didn't have anything that impressed the judge. Could've been the fat thighs that turned him off. Actually I don't think she was smart enough to consider the tactic of trying to influence the judge that way. I'm sure that was the belly-crawler's idea.

I saw a couple of the jurors smiling at the suspect and knew the verdict before it was even read. If any of the jurors from that trial are reading this and you're bright enough to remember all the way to that wonderful year of 1984 … You blew it!

I remember quite well. What I vividly recall is sitting in that courtroom and thinking, *if I'm ever going to go bad … this will be the turning point in my life.*

My friend and I were soon cordially invited to attend an Internal Affairs hearing at the Atlanta Police Department. Detective M.F. Jones of Atlanta's IA unit would be our host.

What we found when we arrived at APD for the hearing was the game room owner from our county that had been punched the same night as the gun incident, along with a lobby full of people who had filed complaints against Officer Allen T. Bailey for various reasons.

We were allowed to tell our story, despite the fact that the officer's belly-crawling defense attorney tried to prevent us from speaking on the grounds that his client had been exonerated in a county courtroom. The exoneration meant nothing at the IA hearing (it meant nothing to us, either). This was a hearing, not a trial.

People took turns describing their experiences with Atlanta's finest. They told of being assaulted, having their vehicles kicked by him in traffic, etcetera, etcetera, etcetera. After all the overwhelming information against this nut-job … all he received was a suspension. Welcome to Atlanta.

Two years later I got a civilian job in the county police department where I lived as a way of continuing to pay for my college courses. I never intended to stay, but I was offered a new position in the department as a CSI. This was before it was chic to be a CSI. I used my artistic skills to do composite sketches for crime victims and scale diagrams of homicide scenes. My duties also included processing crime scenes, collecting and processing evidence, and locating and analyzing latent prints.

I was watching the news one evening in May of 1991 when a picture of Atlanta's finest appeared on the screen. The county police had arrested Officer Allen Thomas Bailey at his Mableton home. He was accused of holding his wife and three-year-old son at gunpoint and threatening to kill them during a domestic dispute. He also threatened to kill anyone who tried to approach the house. For whom do you think that message was intended? His fellow brothers in blue perhaps?

The county SWAT team found Bailey passed out drunk in his house. He was wearing his bullet proof vest when he was found.

If you're expecting me to say something like, "I couldn't believe it," then you'll be waiting a long time. I wasn't surprised at all. Why should I be? I'd seen him do something very similar with my own eyes seven years earlier.

I went to work the next day. I unlocked and entered my work area, which also happened to be the room in which evidence from persons crimes was temporarily held until being transferred to the Evidence Unit. There was a collection of firearms upon the shelving that hadn't been there the day before. I looked at the evidence tags bearing case number 0591-060569, which had been attached to the weapons. I knew what name would be in the suspect block before even looking at the evidence form:

Bailey, Allen Thomas
1140 Gerald Place, Mableton, GA.

My eyes then proceeded directly to a stainless steel Smith & Wesson model 29-3 … serial number N890899. A .44 magnum revolver. I felt about ninety percent sure that this was the same weapon which had been pointed at my friend seven years earlier. Now here I was through such an interesting twist of events looking at the revolver from quite a different perspective.

I hoped that even one of the jurors, the judge, and the people in the court-room during the 1984 trial had seen the news the night before. Should I have taken the actions of the jury personally? Probably not. Did I? Oh, most definitely. I still hold them accountable to this day.

The part the belly-crawler played isn't omitted by accident. I do so just because it would serve no purpose to expect him to display any semblance of a conscience about this. I refuse to even mention his name due to a total lack of respect for him as a person and for the bulk of his occupation. Call me unreasonable.

On December 10, 1991 the following article appeared in the *Marietta Daily Journal* (reprinted with permission):

Atlanta Officer Faces Sentencing

By Jeff Gill/Marietta Daily Journal Staff Writer

An Atlanta police officer faces up to 25 years in prison following his conviction last week in Cobb Superior Court that he pointed a pistol at his wife and threatened to kill her.

Cobb Superior Court jurors on Friday found Allen Thomas Bailey, 35, guilty of aggravated assault and terroristic threats, which carries a total maximum sentence of 25 years in prison.

After he was convicted, Bailey, an 11-year veteran of the Atlanta Police Department, told Judge Robert Flournoy Jr. that he would be suspended without pay while the department conducts a formal proceeding to fire him.

Bailey was accused of holding a gun on his wife, Jacqueline, and 3-year-old son and threatening to kill them during a domestic dispute May 22 at the Baileys' home at 1140 Gerald Place in Mableton.

The jury found that Bailey had held a gun on his wife and threatened his wife, but acquitted him on the charges relating to his son.

Mrs. Bailey told police that her husband had been drinking that day and that he threatened to kill anyone who came near the house. When she took the witness stand during the trial, she testified that her husband did not threaten her or her son.

Police said that shortly after Bailey made the threats Mrs. Bailey walked out of the home and called police. Police called Bailey at his home, but no one answered. Cobb's SWAT team later arrived and found Bailey asleep in the house.

Bailey tried to plead guilty to the incident in a hearing before Judge Flournoy last month. At the hearing, prosecutor Van Pearlberg asked Judge Flournoy to place Bailey on probation for three years and treat him as a first offender.

Judge Flournoy rejected the plea. He said at the time that the allegations, if proven at trial, warranted time in prison.

He said Monday that the evidence at Bailey's trial was "not as aggravating" as the facts laid out at his plea hearing and that he might consider placing him on probation.

Sentencing is scheduled for Jan. 23.

Not exactly the kind of behavior American society should expect from our police officers, but our liberal injustice system operates like this all the time. Only years later did I understand why ... when I was a police officer myself. A courtroom is a liberal playground more often than not. Lawyers, perpetrators, judges, biased jurors. Liberals!

Only after all this activity did this guy finally lose his job as a police officer. He was only a police officer on the surface. More than a uniform and a gun are required to qualify as a police officer in the United States. A heightened sense of humanity and a good heart are necessities. A strong sense of honor and courage are imperative. The rest are just empty shells with uniforms and guns. Bailey was an empty shell.

I obtained police reports in 2006 through Open Records indicating he was arrested in June of 1993 for driving under the influence of alcohol, possession of an open container of alcohol, impeding the flow of traffic, no proof of insurance, and a seat belt violation. His blood alcohol level was .37, which was nearly four times the legal limit at that time and nearly five times the current Georgia standard of .08.

The same Open Records also provided me with a report indicating he was arrested in May of 1994 for criminal trespass and obstruction in the Chattahoochee National Park area at the Cobb and Fulton County border. The report completed by the arresting officers describes some very strange and irrational behavior by the former Atlanta police officer. That description pretty much covers the entire life of Allen Thomas Bailey. Wouldn't you agree ... ladies and gentlemen of the jury?

Progressions in my career found me as the midnight shift uniform sergeant in the western part of the county in which I work by 2001. In June of the following year I responded as the back-up unit for one of my officers who was on a DUI stop at about 2:00 a.m. The officer attempted to conduct field sobriety procedures on the semi-cooperative suspect and then arrested him for DUI and speeding. I began inventorying the suspect's car for the impound form and found a baggie of marijuana and smoking pipe within the console compartment. I brought the find to the attention of the arresting officer, who looked into the car, shook his head and said, "You know who this guy is, don't you?"

"No. Who?"

He told me the arrestee was the son of one of our state court judges, which also made him the son of the belly-crawler who had defended Allen T. Bailey two decades earlier. The world isn't really as small as everyone says it is. The simple connection is disappointingly non-philosophical. One liberal begets another. Belly-Crawler Jr. was allowed to plea to reckless driving … so his arrest wouldn't affect his progression at *law school*. And so the cycle continues.

That story is more personal to me than it would otherwise be simply because of my original involvement as an eyewitness, but this is our injustice system at work. These things happen every day. Conservative members of the system battle for truth, resolution, and appropriate punishment. Liberals fight tooth and nail against these concepts. That stands to reason since they're usually on defense as defendants, defense attorneys, liberal judges, or liberal jurors.

There are many thousands of court proceedings across this nation within a single day. Not all the defendants are guilty of whatever they've been charged. Hopefully the outcomes reflect the truth. Most are guilty, though, and the overwhelming majority are liberals. How do I know this? Because one of the commandments of the liberal bible is *the rules don't apply to you.*

The one ethical defense attorney I've ever seen in action was Ben Matlock. He was unfortunately a fictional character on television, played by Andy Griffith. Matlock believed in and proved the innocence of his clients.

I wonder what percentage of the time the garden variety defense attorney actually believes in the innocence of his or her client. That's a single-digit number without a doubt. They don't care. The injustice system is like our federal tax system … purposely convoluted and bastardized. The system is designed to make money for attorneys. End of story. They make money on those hearings, motions, negotiations, filings, phone calls, photocopies, appearances, trials, etcetera. They get to see every card the prosecution holds before the game even begins. Their job in the majority of cases is to manufacture lies that attempt to stab holes in the prosecution's truths.

The defense attempts to delay things as long as possible in many instances. Through orchestrated postponements and excessive motions the passage of time becomes a tool used to attempt to diffuse the power of solid evidence. A good defense attorney is also always holding onto the hope that witnesses and victims might die if matters are delayed long enough. Matlock sought the truth and cleared his clients from start to finish in less that an hour. What's the problem with the rest of you?

The point is that these people make their living nurturing and selling lies. I believe I'd make an excellent defense lawyer having worked in law enforcement. Cops are involved in many cases from the start, often times witnessing an offense occur and perhaps even catching it on video. I've still seen many times how court proceedings can make *the way things are* eventually become *the way we want a judge or jury to perceive things*. Fact becomes fiction. Truth gets diluted into a brew of lies, because only the defense is allowed to lie. They have to prove nothing. I'd also make a terrific burglar, rapist, murderer, or robber. There are a lot of things I refuse to do for acquisition of money and power. Defending scum in our courts is one of them.

Now let's talk about judges. They're a little different animal than a defense lawyer, although they're connected to the same family tree. There are Conservative judges and liberal judges and they're paid the same. A Conservative defense attorney would be a poor one. Conservative judges wear black robes in mourning for the truth and to conceal their firearms. Liberal judges wear them to conceal their diapers and penis pumps.

One of the better judges in my county once told me at a Christmas party that police officers were "human garbage collectors." I wasn't offended. She was correct. I want all my cases handled in the court of a judge who recognizes that most of the people who appear before her in jumpsuits are waste products. I would add that some of those in business suits also qualify.

A Conservative judge can do a lot of good on the bench. A liberal judge on the other hand is capable of causing an infinite amount of irreparable damage. Either one can run into problems by letting the power go to their heads, but name one occupation where that isn't true.

Liberal lawyers become liberal judges. Liberal judges dispense tolerance and injustice with a weak mind, weak heart, and plenty of arrogance. They're not totally unlike the apathetic parents mentioned in the first two chapters. The word of the day in the court of a left-wing judge is *unaccountability*.

Jurors are representative samples of the population of a given area. What does that mean if the bulk of the lot are card-carrying idiots, though? Attorneys throw bait and jurors run with it like mad carp, having drawn their views on life and the legal system from soap operas.

A juror has a duty to leave their biases and opinions outside the courthouse. He or she is there to basically do what a judge would do in a non-jury trial …

weigh evidence and use unbiased reasoning to make an intelligent determination about a case. Great big fat hairy chance!

Judges typically thank jurors for their attentiveness and service at the culmination of a trial, but are those things really true? Jurors so often seem to be deficient in both of those areas. Go to court and watch what takes place and formulate your own opinions, even without the knowledge of what the prosecution knows but can't use. I'd like to think that justice prevails most of the time, but that's just a fantasy. The penalty paragraphs of our laws are seemingly ignored as watered-down and diaper-filling interpretations of those laws lead to the court's favorite sentence ... *intensive probation*. Oooooh. Scary. Now there's a real incentive to avoid the criminal lifestyle.

In the summer of 2000 I was subpoenaed to serve on the Cobb County grand jury. Being a law enforcement officer didn't excuse me from grand jury service. The only stipulation was that I couldn't listen to cases which had been made by members of my own department. I was therefore constantly in and out of the jury room depending on the agency for which a testifying officer happened to work. Getting selected for jury duty is rarely an exciting prospect for anyone, but I had to do my civic duty just like everyone else there.

Never in my life had I ever been so disheartened about the state of our injustice system than when I served on that jury. Probable cause was eloquently explained to them on day one by a member of the Cobb County District Attorney's Office. I attempted to remind them of that meaning several more times during the term of our service. Some of them just never could grasp the simplicity of our two-pronged duty. We were to listen to synopses of the many cases that came before us and decide two simple things about each to determine probable cause:

a) Was a crime committed?

b) Was the accused probably the person who committed the offense?

If the answer to either question was no, then as a grand juror you don't vote for the indictment. If the answer to both was yes, then you vote for the indictment. This wasn't rocket science, but some of these people just didn't get the idea.

Some of them wanted to try cases right there, asking irrelevant questions that went far beyond the scope of probable cause. Why should these laymen be any different? Defense attorneys are allowed to behave similarly in many probable cause hearings.

Bias came into play many times. One moron refused to vote on any drug case and drug cases composed the majority of the whole. He refused to vote because his *opinion* was that drugs should be legal. Perhaps it was for the best that there were two seats between he and I, because I really wanted to see if he thought a good solid backhand qualified as assault or if that should be legalized, too.

One geezer that had ongoing difficulty comprehending probable cause listened to one segment of testimony and then was more concerned about why the arresting officer had been allowed to use a patrol vehicle on a part-time job than he was about the offense at hand. I'm a restrained and non-impulsive person, but some of the other jurors really began to sense my frustration. Maybe the smoke signals coming from my ears tipped them off.

The last straw came when they didn't want to indict cases of domestic violence simply because some victims came in and testified that they didn't want to prosecute.

"This is precisely why we have domestic violence laws," I fumed. "The victims never want to prosecute and always change their stories! That's part of the cycle of DV situations! The warrant was taken by the officer who investigated the incident, not the victim! The fact that she doesn't want to prosecute is irrelevant!"

I was quite glad when the term of service ended, and when it ended I had to convince myself that I wasn't wasting my time putting effort into my job as a law enforcement officer.

Most officers I hear discuss the issue of court can sever themselves from caring about what becomes of the cases they make. They do their jobs and don't worry about the fact that the courts so often don't do theirs. These officers can say to themselves, *what the courts do is out of my hands.* I've personally never been able to view the matter so lightly and here's why:

Assume you're an artist who paints … preferably one of the rare Conservative artists. Anyway, you complete a terrific work of art that took you six weeks to paint. Behold … a masterpiece. You sell the painting to a buyer who subsequently smashes the masterpiece to bits before your eyes, dusts off his hands, and walks away. The painting was originally yours, but now it's his and he destroys it. That's the way I feel about the injustice system throwing out one of my hard-fought arrest cases just because they didn't want to deal with it.

Is it any wonder that court should be a frustrating experience for a police officer? Most police officers are Conservatives, and what do they see when they go to court? Perpetrators, defense attorneys, and left-wing judges. Liberals! A courtroom is a liberal's playground! A liberal wants to work in the court system, news media, and university system the way a child molester is attracted to the prospect of infiltrating schools, scout troops, and churches. They want to be where the booty is. They desire to be within their comfort zone of power.

My *American Heritage Dictionary* includes the following definitional segments of the word *liberal*:

> **favoring the freedom of individuals to act or express themselves in a manner of their own choosing*
> **morally unrestrained*
> **favoring the use of government power to promote social progress*[2]

How fitting. My interpretation of these descriptions is to picture a ponytail-wearing defense lawyer and his client with their arms around each other's shoulders. They're smoking dope in the courtroom, wearing womens' clothes and loudly declaring, "We plead not guilty to smoking this dope!"

Liberals love the injustice system, where they may go to wash away nasty truths in the diseased waters of lies. The lawyers get paid selling off pieces of conscience and the criminals get their slates cleansed. Kind of sounds like going to confession, except for one missing key element. Truth.

Truth to a liberal goes only as far as the threshold of what may be proven. If something cannot be proven with videotape or some other hard evidence, then it didn't happen. Even if there is videotape, then it must have been altered in some grand conspiracy perpetrated by Conservatives. Look at this part of the definition of liberals again: "favoring the freedom of individuals to act or express themselves in a manner of their own choosing." They follow only those laws convenient to their actions. The rest simply do not apply to them.

Our injustice system convicted Bernie Goetz and acquitted O.J. Simpson. Conservative jurors evaluate evidence presented to them and seek truth, while liberal jurors concern themselves with extraneous factors like race and they vote accordingly. Liberals are more concerned with the legalities of wiretapping than the prospect of snaring terrorists and other criminals.

There are multiple sets of rules in our nation. I'll list them in order from the most to the least restrictive. There's a strict set of largely self-imposed and self-disciplinary rules for Conservatives. There's a set of rules for the average citizen. There's a set of rules for athletes and members of the entertainment industry. The final and least restrictive set of rules exists solely for the Kennedy cult of Massachusetts.

Our injustice system was created to free the innocent and withhold freedom from the guilty. This ultimately became the bastardized system we have today and has become one of routine *injustice*. Everyone is innocent … as long as they're liberals.

◆　　◆　　◆

The following is a darkly humorous little story I wrote years ago to sublimate my frustrations about the injustice system. I wasn't even a police officer yet when I wrote this:

THE SINISTER LITTLE STORY

Sinister McBride led a terrible life.
    As a child he was alone and without.
Every experience sparked a battle inside as to
    which side of him would come out.
A portable halo made an excellent mask, and
    when he had to he'd wear it awhile.
It was a useful disguise on many occasions,
    so masquerading became part of his style.
He knew not what was love, or so he pretended,
    for he turned when chance sent it his way.
Years of practice of turning away made it
    easy for Sinister to hate.
He never committed to anyone or anything, so
    as a young man he knew it was time.
Sinister said, "Dear Money, Dear Power, won't you
    come and be mine? For in your names I'll commit to a crime."
Now, Hanahan's Hot Dog Stand on the street corner was run
    by Mr. and Mrs. Nice.
For thirteen dollars and thirteen cents, Sinister
    carved them up with his knife.
Blood filled the gutter like catsup does a bun
    and very soon the whole town was afraid.
Then the state, the nation, the continent and the world
    heard of the Nice mess that someone had made.
This monster so enjoyed his knife that he
    picked it up each night.
He said, "No one else knows just how it feels to suffer,
    so I'll show them, each one, what it's like."
Lives he took as though they were free in the

shadows of the streets each night.
But a man who saw his eyes in the dark near a killing
  blurted, "He did it! Sinister McBride!"
So the police took him in for questions, but the
  fiend merely told them some lies.
And he asked, "How can you lay this much guilt on a man
  based solely on the identity of his eyes?"
They said, "Oh, Sinister! Your eyes are quite different than most,
  but you're correct, that's just not enough.
Although there's another reason why you're here …
  here and wearing those handcuffs.
You see, the woman you killed along 3rd Street last night knew you,
  for she printed a name before she died.
On the sidewalk beside her in her very own blood
  she wrote SINISTER MCBRIDE."
Caught, he stated boldly, "Yes, I cut up the old bat! Had I known I'd left her the energy
  to write, I'd have chopped off her fingers while at it!"
The public wanted to hang him and the
  policemen felt the same.
But the judge on the case said, "No. Poor Sinister has
  suffered enough. His empty childhood is to blame."
Through the courthouse doors Sinister walked
  with no remorse concerning the slaughter.
Can you imagine how stupid the judge must have felt when
  Sinister married his only daughter?
So justice became the father of Evil … Evil now
  leading two lives.
He continued his role as executioner of the innocent
  and by day he'd return to his wife.
Wait a minute, he thought, now I'm half good, and this
  just isn't working out right.
So he picked up an ax and he woke up his wife
  and took them both into the night.
He remembered a place where he felt invulnerable,
  whispering, "C'mon, honey, let's go up there."
With that he walked his wife up the steps of the courthouse
  and raised the ax high into the air.
Hacking and chopping. Slicing and dicing. Until

morning he continued his realm.
At the end of it all his poor wife had been scattered from
    the courthouse to 3rd Street and Elm.
Sinister was caught, if you can call it that, for
    he didn't even try to run free.
He was so unafraid of the power of the court that
    he readily admitted his deed.
But this time the judge was just, because it was
    his daughter who had been cut to ribbons.
The court found him guilty and the judge called out,
    "Sinister McBride, go to prison!"
So he did, but he liked it there, for nothing
    did he lack.
Everything he had was paid for in taxes by the families
    of the people he'd hacked.
Some said that Sinister should live out his life in the
    prison just like the judge said.
Some said that Sinister should pay with his life.
    "He murdered, so he should be dead!"
If you believe in true Justice rather than that in its
    practiced form,
Then pick up an ax and protect yourself, for each day
    another Sinister is born.
Protection isn't merely defensive.
    Initiative is for societal health.
And if I could reach McBride in that so-called jail cell he's in …
    I'd kill the son of a bitch myself!

by Barry Mason
1988

6

ECONOMICS 101

The going rate for losing a tooth in the early '70s was fifty cents. You put your tooth beneath your pillow at bedtime and awoke with a jagged grin to the jingle of two shiny quarters. This week's tooth fairy listing on the NYSE (symbol: TFY) finds the rate holding steady at five dollars! What else has seen a 1,000% increase during that period? Either we're being scammed today as adults or we were short-changed as children then. I'm considering initiating a class action lawsuit against the tooth fairy for the recovery of back pay. I also smell a rat at home, where my eight-year-old daughter just lost her sixty-fifth tooth.

There's no better way for a child to begin learning the value of money than by paying them an allowance for completing chores. People who earn their way have far more character and positive traits than those who receive handouts their whole lives.

We've probably all known or heard about self-made folks who you would never know had the millions they had earned. We've definitely all witnessed the demeanor of those who have a little more money than the average American and didn't earn it themselves, and yet they behave in a boastful, demeaning, unjustifiably arrogant manner. See that over-the-hill guy next to you in traffic in the convertible sports car, coordinated clothing, and mirrored sunglasses? He doesn't flush. He probably doesn't even wash his hands. Want to make him mad? Don't look at him. See his girlfriend? She's twenty-five years younger than he. What do they do for a living? He's a professional liberal. She's a stripper. He'll be broke within a year and she'll be gone.

There's one very defining factor between Conservatives and liberals when it comes to economics. Liberals cornered the market on lack of work ethic. 'Tis the nature of the Marxist left. Lack of work ethic to a liberal is like a turtle's shell; it surrounds him, defines him, and provides his place of retreat when his surroundings overwhelm his poor little reptilian brain. The only task into which a liberal will put full effort is taking those measures necessary to maintain the liberal life-style. How ironic.

A favorite left-wing topic is discussing the haves and have-nots. Those evil Conservatives promote capitalism and lack of government intervention. In floats Super-lib with the lower-case "l" upon his sunken chest, trying to save the day by making sure everyone has the exact same number of cookies in their sacks. Super-lib loves big government. The more problems he attempts to solve with legislation, the more problems he creates. He stands there upon a street corner in his purple tights and rainbow diaper, shouting anti-Conservative rhetoric to any of the cattle willing to listen. His archenemy with the big "C" on his chest shouts from the opposite street corner, but the crowd he draws is quite different. The "C" crowd knows that everything a business or individual undertakes will typically function with far more efficiency than anything Super-lib attempts through big government. Super-lib is hopping mad. He fills his diaper a little more and tries to incite his whimpering cattle to riot. His archenemy just shakes his head and laughs in unison with the "C" group.

The basic opinion from the Conservative side of the road is that the odds are the haves are haves because they worked hard at successful business ventures, legitimate or otherwise. May the legitimates flourish. May the otherwise group always be discovered and arrested. The Conservatives' contention is that the have-nots are what they are due to one predominant trait. They're lazy! They're too sorry to work and they want the government to take care of them. That's another way of saying that the haves take care of the have-nots.

The liberals holler from their gutter that the haves exploit the have-nots. They whine that capitalism should be replaced by communism. Everyone could then be happy, sit around, smoke dope, and there would never be another war. The only business ventures would be those sanctioned by big government. There would be no need to imprison anyone for anything, because all the prisons would either be torn down or turned into bath houses.

Are there Conservative have-nots? Sure there are, but they're always at least trying to legitimately become haves.

Are there liberal haves? What do you think flaming lefties like John Kerry and Hillary Clinton are? You won't find them waiting in the food stamp lines they so overwhelmingly support. What about ninety-five percent of Hollywood? Their diapers are trimmed in gold leaf.

Are you perhaps wondering about the possibility of liberal haves who obtained their wealth illegitimately? All you have to do is look to their champions. Read a book about the Kennedy clan sometime. Just make sure the book isn't history according to some liberal journalist, otherwise you might not read the parts about bootlegging, organized crime, and murder.

Haves and have-nots indeed. The haves are just those people who are too driven and too smart to be have-nots. The have-nots are just too stupid to be anything else.

This leads us to a brief discussion of welfare. We all know what it is, which is a scam. What welfare *should* be is all but eradicated. Welfare should be for those select few who cannot care for themselves for whatever reason. The welfare liberals wouldn't fare well in the world according to Barry, because the definition of "able-bodied" would be as broad as the sea. You don't work ... you don't eat. You don't eat ... you die.

Many Americans are sick and tired of paying the way for a class of leeches that want to sit on their butts and let the rest of us support their laziness through liberal-imposed legislation. Not only do I want it stopped ... I want a refund!

An interesting concept I've heard about is a charity-based welfare system. Those who wish to give may do so. Those who don't want to raise a leech farm don't have to contribute. I personally don't really care who decides how the money would be distributed. None of it would be mine. I'd rather contribute to the local animal shelter.

Examples of legitimate welfare recipients should be American soldiers permanently injured in battle, orphans, and those select few who are totally incapable of caring for themselves. We're the only species I can think of that labors so insanely to keep our intentional weak links in the chain. If you think that those links should be dropped, then as a fellow contributor I certainly feel your pain.

We got a really good look at the welfare class and the big government that panders to them when in 2005 a really angry lady named Katrina came to New Orleans. Most people probably felt what I initially did upon seeing the reported devastation, which was compassion. Then as the weeks went by we got to see the true side of New Orleans. We saw thugs pillaging their own neighborhoods. We repeatedly heard the angry battle cry of the welfare class, "Where's our checks?" We saw government incompetence in all it did and didn't do.

The welfare mentality. Entitlement. Government incompetence and waste. Ridiculous and inappropriate blame. Corruption. Watching all this unfold I experienced a drastic change of feelings about the Katrina situation. Any compassion I'd had was lost and replaced by rage. I have to remind myself that some hard-working, contributing people lost their lives or property. I can't imagine the sense of loss involved in such a catastrophe.

Many people did ask legitimate questions about why people hadn't left when told to do so, or why they hadn't secured appropriate insurance to offset the constant threat of living along any coast. Only lame attempts to answer such questions were offered. As for the welfare bunch ... many folks ultimately felt like a huge toilet had been flushed when Katrina hit New Orleans. The waste ended up washed into other cities, where they still lounge about hotel rooms at our expense. They've never worked before. Why should they start now?

Liberals don't flush ... but apparently Mother Nature does. *Hey, Mom! Is D.C. too far inland for you?*

Another big government scam throughout the years has been the social security system. How would you feel if you had invested a huge portion of your life-long earnings into Microsoft only to have Bill Gates dip into your investments and squander them on gambling and strippers? Mr. Gates would be arrested and you would be irate. Well that's not far removed from what the federal government has done with our social security money. First of all they hold a gun to your head and force you to "invest." Then they cock the hammer and tell you exactly how much you'll "invest." Kind of sounds like an episode of *The Sopranos*, huh? They've dipped into our savings with their grubby little politicians' hands and redirected funds toward programs of their own choosing. The lot of them should be in federal prison for fraud and theft. They've abused and mishandled working peoples' money and their trust for decades, when we could've been investing both in areas of our own choosing. Actually I think slot machines and strippers would've been better investments than the United States social security scam. Social security is just one more government giveaway program to benefit the bottom-feeders of the nation. Anytime you see the word *social* followed by any word other than *club* is a huge sign of liberal foul play. Once again ... I want a refund, but this time I demand interest! That too I learned from *The Sopranos*.

There has been competition amongst people since Sheeba the cavewoman walked from her hole in the hillside wearing her tiger skin bikini. Og started toward her and Zog clubbed him in the head. The original corporate takeover.

Og's subsequent anti-competition legislation is still carried today on the original stone tablet by modern liberals. "Competition bad," they grunt.

Zog's simple act of raising and lowering his club would of course be illegal today, but in his day he was simply exercising his rights to capitalize within a free enterprise system. Cave paintings indicate that Sheeba wasn't particularly appealing by modern standards. To Zog and Og she was very much worth their competitive efforts. A week later Og beaned Zog with a rock and away he lumbered with Sheeba over his shoulder. She didn't mind. Her value increased with every blow delivered on her behalf. She ultimately left Og and Zog high and dry by marrying an abacus programmer. She got implants, a vacation cave in Shooba-dooh, and a different wheel for every day of the week.

I find myself categorized with a number of Americans who are all for competition, but with a few checks and balances in place to guard against those who might linger along the border of criminal business tactics. We could operate with a capitalistic free-for-all. That system would be what a pure capitalist would want, but many people are too suspicious of the criminal mind to assume that the crooks would be removed in the wash. White collar crooks need to go to prison. The way to make that happen is to give the dog of capitalism as much leash as can be allowed through as little government intervention as possible.

"Competition is good," yell Conservatives.

"Competition is evil," yell liberals.

What stands to reason is that natural born losers would obviously oppose competition. The only way they can get cookies in their sacks would be to steal them or rely on handouts. I don't understand why in this day and age we can't just drop the word *liberal* and call them what they are. *Communists.*

The ridiculous rise in gas prices brings about another issue. What should be done about the rising cost of something that we must have versus other less imperative goods and services? If the cost of a Chick-fil-A sandwich goes to twenty bucks, then we simply cease to buy Chick-fil-A sandwiches. There's a lot of other good food out there from which to choose. We could send a message to Chick-fil-A by ceasing to buy their products. The message would be "get the cost to a reasonable level or we will continue to not purchase your sandwiches. There's a Subway right across the street and we'll go there."

I use those restaurants as examples because I happen to like them both. Who knows? We might actually be paying twenty bucks for a sandwich sooner than we think. I again consider the 1,000% increase in operating costs that the poor tooth fairy has had to absorb. That formula would put the cost of a regular Chick-fil-A sandwich at close to $30.00 after taxes. Twenty dollars suddenly sounds like a really good deal.

"Go ahead and give me the number one combo meal."

"Yes, sir. That will be $50.00, please."

"What a deal!"

There are very few things that we either can't survive without or that we can't replace by making other choices, but what about something like gasoline? They've got us over the barrel on such commodities (no pun intended). Gas is required to make my vehicle operate. I need my vehicle to get to work so I can earn the money to buy the gas. Gas is high everywhere we go, with variations of just a few pennies in most cases.

I could declare that I'm just not going to pay the high costs for fuel anymore. That would leave me with a very short list of alternatives. One would be to steal the gasoline, to which more Americans have resorted in recent years. Gas drive-offs increase as gas prices increase. Most occur because the price increase doesn't fit into the closely cut budgets of the thieves. Some may occur because of anger over the prices. There is no typical drive-off suspect or vehicle. The crime transcends all races and may involve a BMW 750 just as readily as an '84 Pontiac with rust holes. The only consistency amongst the drive-off vehicles seems to be a statistically significant number of faded Kerry-Edwards stickers.

Let's forget theft as an option. You liberals just pretend for a moment. Option number two would be to get a more fuel-efficient vehicle. My Ford F-150 gets a whopping 12 miles per gallon. The truck has two fuel tanks and you can literally watch the fuel gauge needle move from right to left like the 2006 Republican Party. I could get rid of that pickup and easily triple my mileage with one of those currently available motorized insects on the market. I'm thinking that the Scion xB looks like fun. Some say it looks like a shoebox on wheels. I say it's radically cubical. The point is that there are multiple cars available that get mileage in the thirties and cost less that $20,000.00. What we want must in such situations be sacrificed for what we need. I'd really like a blue Dodge Viper with white racing stripes. Folks in hell want ice water. Let's see who gets satisfied first.

Carpooling is terrific, but can quickly lead to various inconveniences. Walking to work is great if you're one of the few people lucky enough to be within a range to reasonably do so. The same holds true for cycling. I wouldn't mind riding a bus to and from work. The problem with that is I'm not poor, so I have no bus route near my home. If I have to drive five miles to catch a bus to a job site that's ten miles from home, then the whole process is a waste of effort. Besides, liberals tend to collect on buses and I elect to avoid them when possible even if they're silent. Those who don't flush also tend not to bathe.

So how do we as a group of people force down the price of gasoline the same way we can affect the cost of sandwiches? Don't take unnecessary trips. Carpool. Work from your homes when feasible. Walk. Cycle. Ride buses. Do all the things already mentioned if they're within the confines of your lifestyle, but for the love of Sunday, don't drive one of those ridiculous urban tanks that gets eight miles per gallon and then complain about gas prices!

The federal government offered a significant tax break on the cost of urban tanks for those who owned their own businesses and then the price of gasoline went through the roof. Coincidence? Maybe. I still smell a rat. How often does the government do anything not designed to feed itself ... the monster?

Talk of a 100-dollar gas voucher from the government is an insult! Screw them and their $100.00. What's that, a week's worth of gas? What they should ethically do is give up the lion's share tax they get on every gallon of gasoline sold. One thing about our wonderful politicians is that whenever they get a tax started they never want to stop it, even the ones they initially assure us are "temporary." Our elected liars have set up the oil companies as the bad guys, when the in-pocket profits for these companies haven't changed. Their costs increased, which caused the prices at the pumps to increase.

If the price of chickens starts to rise, do you think Chick-fil-A will pass that cost onto its customers or just take the hit for us out of the goodness of its heart? The obvious answer is the former, unless you're one of the many cattle who also believe our politicians who blame the oil companies for the high price of fuel. *Mooooo!*

What we should be asking are questions about why an oil company's in-hand profit remains the same despite rising costs at the pumps. Why does the federal government make multiple times the amount in tax on a gallon of gas that the oil company does in profit? How can the government do that and then point its knurled finger at the oil industry? Could it be because people are cattle and are too stupid to investigate the truth rather than accept the twisted words of politicians like Hillary Clinton? Why does oil cost seventy-plus dollars a barrel when it should be half that? Why don't we capture some of the oil in the Middle East to help pay for the war? Why don't we drill in the United States when we know good and well that a tremendous supply lies beneath us? Why do liberals scream about fuel prices and then block drilling in our country?

So many Mexicans have salsa in their crotches over wanting to be US citizens without going through the proper channels. Fine. Why don't we cross the border for a change? Let's go down there, kick their asses, and take over their oil operations. Welcome to America! You're now the fifty-first state of the nation! English is now the language of Mexico. Corona is now on tap as a domestic beer. Oh, and by the way, you still can't come north of the border until you've undergone an identification and medical screening process. Can you feel that, Vicente? Felipe?

We sent men to the moon four decades ago. We have the most powerful military in the world. We have some of the greatest, most ingenious people in the world within our borders. We're so high upon the tip of Maslow's Hierarchy that our biggest worry is often whether or not our television recording devices capture our favorite programs, and yet we have nothing other than gasoline to make our fancy cars go *zoom*? Unacceptable.

A lot of people aren't concerned in the slightest about fuel prices. Perhaps they enjoy paying inflated amounts of their hard-earned dollars for a necessity that costs twice what it should. Perhaps their dollars really aren't hard-earned. Maybe they're paid too much for what they do and they feel guilty. They probably drive urban tanks. Maybe they just don't care. I'm personally willing to do my part for now. The king cab pickup will be retired and I'm getting a commuter car that looks and sounds like an insect. My purpose is not to curb any so-called "price gouging" by the oil companies, but to do my part to stick it up the tailpipe of the government for its hidden *tax gouging!*

Natural gas is another product that has seen ridiculous increases in recent years. We now have new devices to heat the water in our homes that function more efficiently than having a gas hot water tank. The water is heated as it's needed with these new systems. Use a fireplace to assist with home heating if you have one and can find wood that's reasonable (good luck). Put on a sweater. Use electrical heating methods. Sleep with someone. That will probably be your spouse if you're a Conservative. You liberals … whoever … whatever.

Do anything within reason to engage the sellers of life's necessities in competition and life gets better, especially if we can keep the government from the loop. Let the government get involved and watch things go to hell. Liberals grin when that happens. Everyone is happier within their comfort zones.

A long time and a lot of work is required to mold a liberal wad of clay into a Conservative work of art. A Conservative walks with his or her head up, basking in the joy of enlightenment. They're the thoroughbreds of the human race in thought and action.

Liberals are the mongrels who sneak under the fence to pick through the dumpsters and create havoc. They carry a diseased thought process, plagued heart, and putrid demeanor. They try to gain power through numbers, through illegitimate procreation, lying to the cattle of the nation, welcoming illegal aliens with open arms, and government handouts. One thoroughbred remains more valuable than an entire legion of these damned things, though. Consider calling an exterminator instead of pandering to them or electing them to political office. Removing liberals from power is after all the most environmentally friendly act. Do the world a favor.

I live in a predominantly Conservative county. The county is used to having a surplus of funds, regardless of people sometimes questioning the way in which it's run. There are a lot more factors affecting our national budget, though. I mentioned illegal aliens. They've caused tremendous harm to the economic systems of our country. Our health care costs are rising every year. Illegals stress our system of taxation and the job market. They're like termites eating away the very structure of our country. I say figuratively spray them. Our politicians adore the thought of collecting the millions of votes they represent if allowed to remain, so their inactivity, pandering, and head-butting of one another over this issue leaves us without proper representation ... again.

We as citizens can resolve the problem of illegal aliens. Don't hire them! I don't care if your business can't survive without them. If that's the case, then you too are a criminal for hiring them.

We can press our elected officials to insure that the laws already in place regarding immigration are enforced. We can press for stricter laws. I can arrest someone for a felony in Georgia for throwing an egg at an occupied vehicle, but have never been able to get one stinking thing done about the illegal aliens I've encountered. Entering this country illegally or remaining here illegally should be a felonious act that any sworn law enforcement officer in the nation can enforce.

Don't conduct business with people who hire suspected illegals! Builders claim that the cost of a new home would go through the roof (okay, that one was intended) without the cheap wages they pay for illegal labor. Well, Mr. Builder, what were you doing before they came along? The truth is that builders and industries that employee illegals aren't passing their savings onto their customers. They're simply pocketing that money.

Do you think an unethical builder who knowingly buys a stolen $500.00 oven for $50.00 will pass the price reduction onto the home buyer? You don't flush if you believe he will. No. He'll charge the home buyer for the price of a brand new oven. The same holds true for *stolen labor!*

Get this! The police precinct in which I work recently had new carpet installed. A man was contracted to disassemble and later reassemble the cubicles in the building for a fee of $1,700.00. One of the detectives noticed a Hispanic man improperly tugging on a cubicle wall and damaging the connections. The detective showed the man how to properly disassemble the cubicle panels and then advised the contractor what his employee had been doing.

"Those guys aren't my regular workers," replied the contractor.

"They're not? Well who are they?"

"I don't know. I just picked them up on the city square this morning to work for me today."

That's correct. You got it. The county inadvertently paid for illegal labor. They also used some free labor by bringing inmates from the county jail to help move furniture. The carpet installation was most likely a low-bid arrangement, like so many tasks undertaken by government operations. So amongst all this tumultuous activity we somehow got our new carpet installed. You tend to get what you pay for. The carpet wasn't pieced together properly and there were drastic color changes within the hallways. A huge portion of the job had to be redone.

No government work can truly be called government work until it's been low-bid contracted and screwed up at least once, so within those parameters the carpet job was a success.

Hey! Maybe if the liberals get their way then the should-be felons can return to damage our cubicles as US citizens the next time. They will probably be making more than the police officers and eligible for an equal amount of social security benefits. They've already got the health benefits. Unbelievable.

The influx of illegal Mexicans makes me angry. The inactivity and indecisiveness of our elected officials makes me angrier. What makes me the angriest is watching as thousands of Hispanic criminals march upon *our* streets and demand that *our* rights be extended to *them*! They additionally have the nerve to not only wave Mexican flags in our faces, but to disrespect the United States flag by flying it inverted, beneath the Mexican flag, or by destroying our flag. That draws my darker side to the surface of my otherwise calm nature. I feel violence brewing within me and within my country, and I sometimes find myself feeling animosity toward Hispanic people now just because of the possibility that one I see upon the street might be an illegal alien. I don't like feeling that way. I refuse to allow myself to become someone who thinks that way. I have to remind myself that illegals come from all countries, and that I certainly can't identify them just by looking. Still … yesterday was Cinco de Mayo. I had Chinese for lunch and Italian for dinner. I couldn't even bring myself to eat at Taco Bell.

I also mentioned illegitimate procreation as a liberal tactic to obtain political power. I make no differentiation here amongst anyone, from every crack ho who is too ignorant to read this anyway, to you Hollywood starlets who already threw this book against the wall during the foreword. All of you and your sperm donors would have your plumbing removed were the decision left to many of us.

Permits are required for everything under the sun anymore. You almost can't blow your nose without getting permission from the government by paying a fee and getting licensed. We're permitted before we can drive. We have to get business licenses to operate our own businesses. We have to get permits to hunt and fish. Sometimes we even get permits to burn refuse on our own property.

I theoretically propose that people should have to obtain pregnancy permits. The human riffraff that run around creating child after child with whoever is willing to lie down are the most dangerous creatures on the face of this planet. Their irresponsible and costly actions produce not only financial burdens, but burdens of every imaginable type. Their actions can be equated to an aggressive cancer that eats at the entire body. They play biological, social, and economic Russian roulette … except the muzzle is pointed at the entire nation.

If these people have to be licensed to carry firearms, then they should most certainly need permits for pregnancy. The latter is potentially by far the most destructive when wielded carelessly. I find raising my own children to be quite a financial strain sometimes. Very much worthwhile, but a strain nonetheless. The last thing I want or need is to have to financially kick down through liberal legislation to the bastards of the poor. Nor do I wish to be victimized by the future political aspirations of the rich ones. *Snip-snip*!

I used to complete my own income tax forms. I was single, owned my own house, and had one job. One year I decided to pull the previous year's forms and use them as a guide for completing the forms for the current year. In so doing I made an error, because the lines had been moved into different positions on the federal form. The error wasn't large, but was $150.00 in my favor.

Three years later I got a phone call from an IRS representative that sounded like she was about twelve years old. The IRS wanted its $150.00. I couldn't believe my ears. I pulled my tax records while the caller waited and I saw the error which she'd brought to my attention. That seemed like a good opportunity to complain about honest people having to pay taxes to this ridiculous extent while illegals and other crooks paid little to nothing. The twelve-year-old didn't care. I mailed the IRS $150.00 and over a decade later still marvel at the injustice.

We all see the enormous bites the government takes from our paychecks. Most of us have thought how wonderful life would be if we got to take home what we actually earned instead of the piece the government doesn't steal.

In 2005 I read *The FairTax Book* by Neal Boortz and Congressman John Linder. I wasn't familiar with the details of a national sales tax until then. The book wasn't the typical boring economics lesson. The ideas were presented in a simplistic format with interjected aspects of entertainment and humor. The bottom line was that the FairTax made sense. The FairTax would be a far superior system to the ridiculously complex, unequal, and corrupt tax code under which the IRS bullies us every year. What system wouldn't?

The FairTax is a consumption tax, not an income tax. Income tax would be discontinued if the FairTax bill could pass. You would get to take home every dollar you earn! What in the world couldn't be good about that? We would pay a sales tax of just over twenty percent on the new goods and services we buy, but people would learn about embedded taxes hidden within the things we buy now if they would read *The FairTax Book* or log onto www.fairtax.org. Those embedded taxes would be eliminated with the passing of the FairTax bill and prices would drop. Businesses not dropping their prices would find themselves floating upon icebergs in the cold sea of failed businesses, thanks to the competition that the left so despises.

So you get your entire paycheck. Every dollar. You decide how much tax you pay simply by making purchases. The sound theory of the FairTax is that an item currently costing a dollar would soon cost around eighty cents following the removal of embedded taxes. Then you purchase that item under the FairTax system, resulting in a cost that would be about one dollar.

There would also be monthly prebates from the federal government to cover a family's basic life necessities such as food.[3] That's correct. You liberals should feel right at home with that idea even if none of the rest of this makes any sense to you. A monthly check from the government. That idea is better than sex to most lefties.

There are other questions about the FairTax that can easily be satisfied by reading the book or visiting the Web site. So who wouldn't possibly want to support replacing our current mess with a national sales tax?

1. There are those who support a flat tax. No thanks. That's still an income tax.

2. Some support the idea of having a "value added tax." Read about that deal in *The FairTax Book* or investigate the VAT on the Internet. The VAT deal is not a good deal.

3. Many people who enjoy the life of sitting on their asses and not working also oppose the FairTax. The hang-up of that network of liberals is directly connected to the fact that all they know of the national sales tax is what their political mongrels tell them. In other words … they're too stupid to read and understand for themselves.

4. Another group of people who oppose the FairTax concept are those benefitting from the corruption of the current system. They're the few who have been playing the current system and winning. Naturally they don't want a change to a fairer tax code. Their attitude is basically, "Screw the rest of you! I've got mine!"

5. The last and most despicable members of the FairTax opposition I'll
    mention are closely connected with those listed under numbers 3 and 4
    above. They're the politicians who are either too ignorant to compre-
    hend the bill or too corrupt to sign it. Some of them are fence riders
    who habitually wait on important issues before committing. That way
    they can protect their own butts and their jobs. Some politicians oppose
    the FairTax bill because it's the product of forward-thinking Conserva-
    tism. This attitude is, "A liberal didn't propose the idea, so therefore it
    must be a product of the evil right. That's what I'll tell the cattle as I
    herd them to the slaughter of financial dependence." *Moooooo!*

At least with a national sales tax the illegal aliens in this country would be
forced to pay their equal share, until we can round them up and return them to
whatever underbrush from which they crawled.

Furthermore, no part-time IRS clerk would call me about a $150.00 error on
a three-year-old tax return. Neither the IRS nor the form would exist with the
FairTax in place.

I can hear the left's welfare class out there bellowing, "What about us?"

If I were sympathetic to your self-imposed plight, then I'd suggest reading ...
sorry ... having someone read to you the eighth and ninth chapters of *The Fair-
Tax Book*. I'm not sympathetic, though. You like living under corruption? Move
to Mexico. I'd gladly trade you one-for-one to Felipe Calderón for some of the
illegal aliens he continues to send north. At least on alien can be trained to flush.

7

CHARGE IT TO MY RACE CARD

Hello. My name is Barry Mason. I'm a heterosexual European-American male Christian from a predominantly vanilla city.

Didn't that sound asinine? Well, asinine is the in-thing and has been for decades. Chicness can readily be found in America by using extraneous factors like race, ethnicity, religion, and sexual preference to express individuality. Other reasons for capitalizing on such issues are to try to use them as stepping stones either to get ahead or to avoid accountability for wrongdoing. Any merited claims of discrimination are lost within the countless cries of wolf. The need to be considered an underdog is a national epidemic.

Use of the N-word was quite prevalent when I was in high school, but not within the parameters of one race to another. Friends used the N-word to greet and address one another and regardless of race it was thrown about as casually as hello. The word was recklessly used with an intended and yet misguided sense of humor.

That misguidance overtook me one afternoon when a classmate gave me a friendly jab to the shoulder as he headed to his seat. The N-word sprang from my mouth with jest and without thought. This classmate happened to be of east Indian descent and his reaction was one of anger and hurt. I was very ashamed of myself. I realized that the origins of the word were not rooted in humor and made a conscious effort to remove it from my vocabulary. I wasn't a racist and didn't want the reckless use of such a word to affect me or those around me like that ever again. The human tongue is a powerful weapon. A lot of people who scream "free speech" need to be reminded that there are limits, just as the left needs constant reminding that "free country" doesn't translate into authorization to do whatever they please.

The N-word can predominantly be heard these days as it frequently escapes the lips of young blacks *and* young whites. Place partial blame upon the rap and Hip-Hop clowns for both or explain why we shouldn't.

Race today should be treated as little more than a feature of identification, just like gender, height, weight, etcetera. Liberals don't want that treatment of the issue, though. They do so love their decks of race cards.

Fifty years ago something had to be done to combat racism. Something *was* done. Everyone sees racism through their own eyes and with their own sets of interpretations. No one can claim that racism wasn't a problem fifty years ago. The Civil Rights Movement was effective and has been successful in bringing us the equality we have today. The problem is that racism didn't disappear; it has simply been evenly spread about the country like a generic margarine. The only racism and bigotry I see now occurs in the forms of an outdated affirmative action and in false claims of discrimination.

I took the advice of Martin Luther King and chose to oppose racism in a non-violent way. My way is sublimation. I write. My 2000 fiction novel *Maroon* contains a chapter in which a police detective (not me!) voices his opinions about the federal government's affirmative action hiring procedures. My 2006 fiction novel *Killswitch* has a character that's a minister named Joseph Salter. Salter and his followers form an organization called the Knights of Racial Indifference. The KRI goes on a cross-country trek to stamp out racism in *all* its forms, not just the traditional ones. The KRI opposes affirmative action as adamantly as they do the Klan.

I know a lot of black people, but I don't think I've ever met a single soul that I would consider "African-American." I'm not called "European-American" just by the trait of being white, so the hyphenated phrase African-American deserves no different treatment as related to people of color who have lived here all their lives.

People just can't let go of the prejudicial chips on their shoulders long enough to look at racial differences, shrug and say, "So what?"

I want to scream at them, "Grow up! Get over it! Let go of your issues and learn to flush!" What the country needs is a good case of amnesia, and don't tell me that those who forget history are doomed to repeat it. We're people, so we'll eventually figure out a way to screw up everything one way or another.

I considered calling this chapter The Big Business of Being Hyphenated. That scope was far too narrow. Being female, Hispanic, or gay have also been thriving business ventures in recent years.

I thought about using the heading The Big Business of Being a Minority. That would work! Ultimately I decided to use the popular phrase "race card" to represent all extraneous issues that people attempt to employ to their advantage.

Toting the race card within the parameters of this chapter refers to all races, nationalities, sexual orientations, and both genders. So why is it acceptable in America to yell "racism" and "discrimination" as long as you're anything other than a straight white male? Could the reason be habit? Dependence upon unaccountability? Minds diseased by liberalism? Yes on all accounts. The problem is just a plain old failure to flush.

Everyone who isn't a straight white male can easily find a so-called protected group of people which they can join to support them in their need to be considered underdogs.

Picture this:

The time is 3:00 a.m. You're a police officer and you observe a vehicle with its lights off moving slowly behind a shopping center. You drive toward the vehicle, at which time its lights come on and it hurriedly begins to leave the area. You were taught in the academy that such a situation is referred to as "suspicious," so you decide to do your duty and check the vehicle to make sure no crimes have been or were about to be committed.

You conduct a traffic stop on the vehicle a short distance from the shopping center. The vehicle pulls over and you use your 747 landing lights to illuminate the passenger compartment. You can't see inside the vehicle due to the hour of darkness and the windows of the vehicle are also dark.

This is what makes a traffic stop dangerous, you think to yourself. You get out and walk toward the vehicle, trying to use your flashlight to see through the side windows. They're tinted. The driver finally rolls down his window when you yell for him to do so over the volume of his stereo. You carefully move alongside the vehicle, still not knowing if there is a gun pointed at you right now or if the vehicle simply contains an employee of the shopping center who worked late.

You finally get a look inside the vehicle and see that no one but the driver is inside, at which time he sneers at you and barks, "What the hell did I do this time? You're just stopping me because I'm black!"

This kind of scenario occurs constantly in police work. The left just doesn't like authority figures and its card-carrying members drop accusations like this automatically. What I withheld from you about this scenario is the fact that you, the officer, are black! You think this hasn't happened? Think again.

Liberals are so much in the habit of playing the role of the falsely disadvantaged that they don't think before they pull the triggers on their mouths.

Consider the actions of Georgia embarrassment Cynthia McKinney in early 2006. Well ... wait a minute. I'll have to be more specific than that, since she's made a horse's ass of herself on more than one occasion lately.

Everybody has probably heard by now the story of how this leftist lunatic assaulted a police officer at the Capitol. She reportedly attempted to bypass security while not displaying her appropriate identification and failed to stop when the officer ordered her to do so. The officer attempted to stop her, at which time McKinney was said to have struck him. Liberals quite often act before they think. McKinney did so when she assaulted the officer. She did so again when under political and criminal fire she attempted to cash in one of her many race cards. The card was denied! Rejected! Over its limit!

The left complains that black females can't get a fair shake in modern society. Oh, really? Being a black female is in actuality a double scoop of the social underdog flavor. They can write their own tickets in many markets of America simply by being black females. Some employers are afraid not to hire them even when they're not qualified. Others may be afraid to discipline them when relevant. The result is that negligent retention is rampant when termination should occur. The reason for such injustices is because of the beloved race card.

The offset is that most people who constantly cash in their race cards will never be successful at whatever they attempt. They in effect keep themselves down. Want to find examples of successful black females who are valued members of the American work force? There are a lot of them. Look for those who simply present themselves as *people* rather than as *black females*. That same formula holds true for everyone else ... even Asian-lesbian-senior-citizens-with-disabilities-who-support-the-humane-treatment-of-wombats (ALSCWDWSHTOW?).

There are exceptions to the rule, as always. Some people make a very fine living being racists, although I would propose that these people are not successful contributors to the work force. They might have fame and money, but their attributes and behavioral patterns make them the fleas upon the ass of the dog. Cynthia McKinney would be one of these. Others would be those who vote for her.

O.J. Simpson and his show-pony lawyer Johnnie Cochran represent America's poster boys for effective tactical placement of the race card weapon. The Mark Fuhrman and crime scene investigation issues certainly didn't help matters, but they really were irrelevant. Race was manufactured into what appeared to be a relevant issue. The jury then bought the product and paid full price in the process.

Juries are manufactured by the lawyers and therefore aren't a true representation of the population. How can anything be true and accurate with lawyers pulling the strings of the process? Throw in the fact that this case occurred in California. Stir in some liberal jurors, some hyphenated mindsets, and ta-da! A prefabricated not-guilty verdict.

How do you think those jurors sleep at night when the truth has to exist in the backs of their minds? I'm sure they sleep just fine. A disconnected or nonexistent conscience is a trademark of much of the left. A lib attempts to compensate for his shortcomings by saving a tree from a chainsaw.

What if O.J. Simpson had been white and Mark Fuhrman had been black? Interesting.

Former Atlanta Mayor Bill Campbell tried his race card in his trial. To say how much the tactic helped him is difficult. There certainly was a lot of talk of his corruption while he was in office and yet he was not found guilty of those charges. He was only found guilty of tax evasion. Kind of reminds me of Al Capone for some reason. Perhaps he too was innocent of matters of corruption.

New Orleans Mayor Racial Ray Nagin requested that people return to the city following hurricane Katrina … so they could insure that New Orleans remained a "chocolate city." He recently was re-elected. Either Katrina didn't wash away all the scum or there has been a significant collection of refuse in the backwash. Way to go, Chocolate City. You would've run out Nagin on a rail if he'd been white and made some idiotic comment about the need to turn New Orleans into a "vanilla city." I had to remind myself that racists support other racists. Hence the re-election. New Orleans, you're no different than the Tom Metzgers of the world. I personally wish that all the leeches still living in hotel rooms around the country would hurriedly return to the Chocolate City. Hurricane season will soon be upon us again.

My mother worked as a dispatcher for a locksmith during the aftermath of Katrina. She took a call from a woman who needed her car unlocked and gave the woman the price and response time. This woman was pleased with neither. She wanted her car unlocked for free because she was "from New Orleans." She also boldly proclaimed that the response time would be much quicker if she'd been a white female rather than black.

The company my mother worked for did respond to the call and unlocked the car for the appropriate fee, which is more courtesy than I would've extended. I would've hung up the telephone after the words "New Orleans," robbing this racist of her chance to swipe her race card.

This woman did later call my mother back to apologize for her comments, to her credit. I can't be as forgiving about such incidents. She was an adult and her true beliefs had been exposed earlier. I'd like to think that she went home to the hotel room for which we're all paying, sat down, and reflected on her need to prop herself upon the crutches of liberalism. I'd like to imagine she threw them away, but I don't hold out much hope.

On 10-26-05 former professional baseball player Joe Morgan complained in *USA Today* that the Houston Astros had no "African-American" players.[4] I couldn't believe my eyes! Where is it written that every group of people in every nook and cranny of the country must possess a member of every race? There weren't any whites in the Jackson 5. Should we have complained? Being hyphenated means it's okay to be a racist as long as you're *not* white. I feel strongly that the tide may be starting to turn on that fashionable trend. I truly hope so. I'd like to see a truly colorblind nation. Not a chance as long as we've got fine American bigots like Bill Campbell, Racial Ray Nagin, Cynthia McKinney, and all their supporters.

USA Today was kind enough on 11-01-05 to print my letter in response to Joe Morgan's ridiculous comments. My letter also wasn't the only one firing back:

MORGAN CRIES 'WOLF' ON BLACK PLAYERS

I sneered reading the article discussing that "the Houston Astros are the first World Series team in more than a half-century with a roster that doesn't include an African-American player" (Astros first Series team since '53 without black player," Oct. 26).

Hall of Famer Joe Morgan was quoted as saying he'd noticed this about the Astros. Morgan also said it's a "predicament and a challenge for Major League Baseball" that there aren't more black players.

Why is this a predicament and challenge? Is it a predicament there aren't more white basketball players or heavyweight boxing champs? That kind of thinking keeps racism alive and breeding like rabbits.

There should be neither racial omission nor favoritism. The same holds true for gender, nationality and any other extraneous factors centered on entitlement.

Crying "wolf" regarding racism has become a monstrous and runaway industry.

The last paragraph of the letter was cut by an editor, so I'll include it here:

There's been a lot of press about the recent passing of Rosa Parks. She obviously had a legitimate complaint. That was pure racism, but the affirmative-action-like mindset that there should be more blacks on a sports team is just as pure.

Hey, Joe, get your race out of my face!

NBA players had apparently dressed like gutter thugs long enough and in 2005 somebody in power got tired of the image they projected. The decision was handed down that they would have a dress code and some of them got together and proclaimed that was racism. A dress code is by that rationale acceptable for everyone around the globe, unless you make your living bouncing an orange ball and throwing it through a hoop. The Constitution of the United States and the Bill of Rights do after all specifically mention the right of all basketball players to wear their pants halfway down their asses.

America is growing tired of hearing people cry "race" when something doesn't go their way … unless of course your name is Jesse Jackson, Al Sharpton, et al. Those of you who present yourselves as *black athletes* instead of just *athletes* are part of what keeps racism alive and well.

Understanding why a basketball player would claim racism when told he'll have to dress presentably rather than as a street urchin isn't difficult. Such a claim is a commonplace ploy in America to secure wants, avoid accountability, and shift blame.

In late 2005 White Sox manager Ozzie Guillen was praised not for winning the World Series, but for being the first Latin manager to do so. Someone is constantly being hailed as the first of some group or another to accomplish something.

My fiction novel *Killswitch* describes the election of the first black US President. His name is Farrish Terrigan and he gains the favor of the people of the nation by being straightforward, and by running as a man … not as a *black* man. The same formula could be extended to a potential female President.

There's a reason why that aspect of *Killswitch* may forever remain fictional. People can't forget their prejudices long enough to realize that their thinking is skewed. The playing of the race card has become like a left wing video game. I've got good news and bad news. The good news is that racism in America has changed drastically since the days of Rosa Parks and Martin Luther King. The bad news is that racism and bigotry are as strong as ever.

I state again that people tend to see racism though their own eyes rather than looking at the big picture. I don't see evidence of white supremacists within my daily environment, but that doesn't mean the morons aren't out there. The racism I personally witness is exercised through affirmative action procedures, negligent retention of members of select groups, almost any cause undertaken by the NAACP, and peoples' voting patterns. I hear racism in the words of liberal politicians as so-called minorities like Racial Ray Nagin spout anti-white rhetoric, or as New York communist Hillary Clinton constantly tries to pander to any self-proclaimed underdog of the month.

I hear racism in the words and see racism in the eyes of people I encounter on my job, who can be lightning quick in making the personal allegation that they're being "harassed" because of their race.

A white male once alleged that the reason I issued him a traffic citation was because he had an out-of-state license plate. Yeah … it had nothing to do with the fact that the plate was *expired*.

Another white male lefty situated within an overrated subdivision along the western border of my county complained that we had "harassed" him just because we didn't make much money and had contempt for "young whites with money." He wanted to ignore the fact that he'd been drunk and disorderly in his own little heavenly golf community. Way to go, moron. Why not return to UGA to get your "liberal arts" doctorate? You're already a master.

The wife of a Hispanic man once informed me that we were "harassing" her husband just because he happened to be Hispanic. This allegation was made as he failed miserably in his American debut at field sobriety procedures. Well, ma'am … I didn't dislike your husband because he was Hispanic. I did dislike him because he was an illegal alien and drunk driver, and I disliked *you* because you were a liberal racist.

People like this cannot be given the pass of simply being referred to as bigots. They're not merely bigots. Each and every one of these people would love to have the entire country populated by no one other than the members of their races … or whatever.

How can someone in my position endure years of such allegations without becoming the hate monger that most liberals believe every person with a badge to be? Conscious effort. Everyone I meet gets a clean slate. From that point on I treat you the way you treat me, up to the point that you start with the racism. I don't take that bait. I simply allow you to wallow in your own failure to flush.

The left adores the word *harassment*. The word gets them so excited that I imagine they scream it aloud during sex, but I doubt the sheep get it.

Racism works in all directions. Why is everyone so shocked over the release of tape recordings of Dekalb County, Georgia, Police Chief Louis Graham and Assistant Chief R.P. Flemister making racist remarks or plotting racially motivated moves within their department? If the disbelief is because of their upper echelon positions, then that's misplaced disbelief. Should we be surprised that Dekalb CEO Vernon Jones may be heading a county that discriminates against whites? The majority of the discriminatory acts that are perpetrated in America are by people holding positions similar to these men. Hopefully the shock is not because Graham and Flemister are black and were recorded making comments like "white boys" and "white bitch."[5] Oh, please. I'll be so bold as to toss out the estimate that just between blacks and whites the ratio of racial offenses (verbal and otherwise) is around 70/30, with blacks committing the higher. Such numbers will of course vary by location and who you ask. That might be an interesting poll to conduct.

Nine times out of ten when I overhear the N-word it's spoken by a black, but again I'll state that this is life within my environment. Other peoples' experiences will obviously vary. Answer this question, though. Why is it that the predominant number of racist comments and false claims of racism are both committed by liberals?

Catch a few bars of rap sometime as one of our young liberals drives by, peeking between the top of his car door and the brim of his crooked hat. You'll have to cover your ears if you find the glorification of murder offensive, or words like "nigger, bitch, fuck, ho ..."

The race card is worn out. The account is overdrawn. Non-racist America awaits the closing of that account and affirmative action with it.

Everyone has at some time said or at least thought offensive concepts. What distinguishes people from one another is how they resolve those ideas, how they wish to be perceived, and how they treat one another. I personally do care what people think of me within reason. The last thing I'd want to do is offend a good person whose opinions and feelings are worth valuing. As for the world's bigots and those liberals who live to swipe their race cards ... this courtesy is coldly not extended to them.

One of my favorite talk show personalities is Herman Cain. He happens to be black. So what? He doesn't promote the riding of the government's coattails and doesn't sell his ideas as a *black man* ... just as a man. His drive and business sense obviously carried him to his very respectable position in life. Those characteristics and a strong Conservative backbone are his selling points. Cain also adamantly supports the FairTax bill. Any office to which he could be elected would be very well served.

Every devout liberal is constantly on the lookout for anything that can be twisted into some sort of special interest disrespect. Years ago a metro Atlanta area police agency had acquired advertising space on a large billboard to showcase members of its various units. The billboard was a beautiful display. A representative of the police department was being interviewed about the billboard by a prominent female Atlanta reporter. She turned to the billboard amidst the interview and asked the officer something like, "Why are there no women on the billboard?"

In the words of the great Ronald Reagan … "Well, there you go again."

Only a liberal would've even noticed that the row of officers on the board were men. Conservatives saw police officers. This reporter saw the absence of women. Perhaps the billboard should've displayed hermaphroditic mulattos who happened to be police officers. That way our devout liberals could turn their attention to something else on which to nitpick. There were no midgets on the billboard either. That must ultimately be some form of heinous discrimination that could only be traced to an evil and dungeon-dwelling Conservative. If this reporter could compose a billboard of evil and dungeon-dwelling Conservatives, then they would most assuredly be all men and that would set easily on her stomach.

I work in law enforcement. That means that I not only work in an occupation where the jobs are held primarily by men, but men who are the more extraverted and Type-A personalities. That doesn't mean all of them walk around constantly wired and on edge. My belief is that some of the best officers are those who carry themselves with the switch set to Type-B, but who can flip that switch to Type-A and back as needed. They're capable of handling the entire array of situations their job can throw at them, with no more turmoil than is necessary for resolution. The occupation would chew up an actual Type-B introvert and spit him out. Hopefully those are eliminated during their departments' hiring or training programs and not upon the streets of America. The point is that there's a lot of testosterone flowing through the veins of the country's police precincts. That's the excuse I use for my hair falling out anyway.

I've heard numerous male police officers through the years state that they didn't believe women should be officers. They cited their reasons, but the primary one I recall is that women just weren't by nature physically or emotionally up to the task. Some said that the overwhelming majority of the women of law enforcement were just plain crazy.

My response to the latter is that all police officers are a little bit nuts just for wanting to do the job. We've got the public, the courts, and our own administrations against us much of the time, and yet many of us stay. That anyone ever retires from a full career in this occupation will always amaze me.

As for whether or not women are physically and emotionally capable ... I've worked with several female officers thus far in my career who were far more capable than some of the males. I'd gladly work with them again and would rather have most of them as a partner than an out-of-condition male ROAD officer (Retired On Active Duty).

Do I think the ratio of good to poor female officers is the same as for the males? Yes. There are simply a lot fewer females and they stand out.

Do I think that female officers are given a wider margin of consideration than males regarding hiring procedures, discipline and retention issues, and in obtaining the more sought-after positions? Yes. Departments tend to consider them less expendable than males thanks to the affirmative action mindset of America. Making your way on your own merit is an ancient philosophy.

I think it's just peachy that Danica Patrick can drive an Indy car. I just don't see the fact that she's a female having any relevance whatsoever. Certainly not to the degree the media obviously believes her gender to be. Surviving and achieving on one's own merit doesn't include such extraneous factors. Let it go.

My middle school class took a trip to Washington, D.C. in the late 1970's. The trip was fast-paced because we had so much to see within just a few days. My memories of the trip therefore lie within my brain like scattered shards, but I recall going to an indoor firing range and watching a person fire a gun at a target. I think my memory is correct in that we were behind a glass partition that separated us from the firing lanes.

The shooter wore some kind of a helmet and put some well-placed rounds within the bull's-eye of the target. We were marveling over the simple process of watching the firing of the weapon, as most twelve-year-olds would do. What really cemented the scene into memory was when the shooter turned to face the audience and removed the helmet, causing her long hair to fall free. She was a beautiful woman if memory serves me correctly. I don't know. Maybe that's just the way I want to remember her.

That was a stroke of recruitment genius on someone's part, which means recruitment must have been farmed to a private company rather than being handled by the government. The scene had quite an impact on the viewing adults and children alike. I still think that was a terrific presentation. Something just feels all wrong about why it should've had such an impact.

A white male and a black female are candidates for the same job. Who should get the position? The person more qualified for the job. The United States is the greatest country in the world, at least for now, but Utopia it is most definitely not. Every staunch Conservative seems to be seeking a way to make our country better. Every staunch liberal seems to be seeking ways to tear her down.

I have absolutely no experience with a homosexual person attempting to swipe their card to either bail from trouble or take an unjustifiable step ahead of the crowd. Everyone has seen, heard, or read about gays in the news who try to shove their preferences to various forefronts.

There was a period of time when you couldn't blow your nose without having to hear about so-called "gay rights." Do you want to know what a gay right is? The same rights everyone else has. Beyond that you would be just another liberal trying to capitalize on a trait that falls outside personal merit. Liberals thoroughly despise words like *personal* or *individual.* Everything is about the *group*. So says Karl Marx.

I recently saw an article about a gay football player who talked about his hidden life within the sports league. Nothing is an issue until it's formulated into one. He's a gay football player. I'm a heterosexual cop. I refuse to acknowledge that either deserves an entire page of a newspaper … unless I get to have my picture taken with the women of my choice. Do they make a 100-page newspaper?

The last time I felt thoroughly violated by the left on this issue was when movie critics and promoters told us every waking minute of our lives just how wonderful the movie *Brokeback Mountain* was destined to be. I've been to Wyoming twice. I saw black and brown bears, deer, elk, buffalo, moose, and Asians. What I didn't see were two cowboys riding hand-in-hand into the sunset.

Jake Gyllenhaal isn't who I imagine when I say, "Howdy, partner." I'd rather see Gretchen Wilson when I open that barn door. Hat on or hat off, darlin'. 'Tis up to you.

I didn't see *Brokeback Mountain*. I don't wish to view that content and I really don't like the fact the critics were trying to shove the movie into our faces. Tush, my dear lefties! I instead went to see *Walk the Line* and *The Chronicles of Narnia: The Lion, The Witch and the Wardrobe*. Both were classically excellent and neither tried to convince me to put a rainbow tag on my pickup truck. If I want to see a couple of dudes roll around together on the floor, then I'll watch a UFC match.

The issue of gay marriage has been in the forefront lately. There's no sense in stating why I disagree with that proposal. I'll just state that I do disagree with it for personal reasons. The reason I choose not to analyze the matter further is because we have about a million more important issues on our plates in this world right now.

Other people who occasionally try to swipe their cards of self-promotion are the handicapped. Who was that golfer that tried to get the PGA to authorize his use of a golf cart during matches because of his handicap? I don't recall. He plays far better than I could even without the use of a cart, but the point is that rules are rules. The human element is never to be forgotten when applying rules, but neither is common sense.

I originally held a couple of civilian positions within my police department until I took the oath to become an officer. One was as the department's sole Crime Scene Investigator, but the first position I had was to handle the warehouse area of the Supply Unit. That job at times required some heavy lifting and moving.

I was asked to help select my replacement before leaving the Supply Unit to be the CSI. I decided that whoever replaced me needed to at least be able to load and unload cases of copier paper using the unit's hand truck and cargo van. That was the most strenuous of the routine heavy lifting. The person would also need decent organizational skills and should understand the basics of ordering and distributing inventory.

Only one person who wanted the job could perform the required tasks at an acceptable level. Pat took over my former position in 1990 and still holds the job today. *She* happened to be the eldest of those who tried for the position. She was the most qualified for the position and she got it. You would never know by Pat's work or her attitude that she has only one leg.

8

REPUBLICAN VS. DEMOCRAT

Point to a communist country that has ever been successful. There's a reason why there haven't been any. The system sucks!

Communism works great for the few in charge, but for the masses it either appeases the lackadaisical or turns the motivated into the lackadaisical. Communism was meant to be limited to parties of no more than ten who happen to be lost in the wilderness. Hmm. Lost in the wilderness. I'd say that perfectly describes the Democratic Party. Unfortunately the description seems to apply more and more to the Republican Party every year.

The Democratic Party has been run like an episode of *Jackass* for years, but especially so after the shock of 9/11 began to wear off. Quite suitable is the fact that the party symbol *is* an ass. You really can't tell from which end Democrats speak anymore.

The Republican Party symbol is an elephant. Elephants are known for their capacity for memory. Republicans therefore need a new mascot, because a great many of them seem to have forgotten their roots. They've spent our money like crazy trying to placate the same bottom feeders who voted against them in 2004 and who will vote against them again in 2008.

You Republicans take notice! You think you can stay in power by playing to the welfare pets that belong to the left? You're wrong! They will gladly accept our money as long as you're tossing it their way, but their liberalism is so ingrained that they would vote for Satan if he were on the Democratic ticket. The other thing you should know is that people like me are turning on you also. Republicans no longer represent core Conservative ideals, so away with you.

Republicans have proven that Conservatism is like religion. There can be backsliding. There will be backsliding. There has been backsliding.

I was joking about Satan running for office as a Democrat. He's got plenty of underlings filling those roles for him. Besides, he's far too busy personally overseeing his Middle Eastern operations against the US and Israel at this time. The only break he's taken since before 9/11 was the time he spent in bed sulking after the 2004 election, as did so many of his underlings.

The basis of the political-social war of which I speak is Conservative vs. liberal, not Republican vs. Democrat. The Republican Party has in the past been the gathering ground for Conservative ideals. The Democratic Party has been the same for liberals. So why does there seem to be a fusing of the actions of the two parties, while at the same time they feud bitterly? Because there are growing numbers of people in the United States who are willing to let the government be their sugar daddy and all those greedy little politicians from both sides want those votes.

Our government has therefore forsaken the rest of us to go after the support of those with the growing numbers ... the bottom-feeders. Politicians in short care more about staying in power than they do about the citizens who actually contribute to society. Government used to be *the people*, but it has become a monstrous entity. The government is becoming Goliath and we're the David. The time has come to cast our stone against the forehead of big government.

How do we do that? By voting out every single one of our representatives who don't have our interests in the forefront. The time is right for a third party to receive some serious consideration and support. Maybe even a fourth and fifth. I don't agree with all concepts of the Libertarian Party, but perhaps they deserve one four-year opportunity to show us what they've got. That would be a difficult task for them, since it would take at least that long for some of the aftereffects of prior regimes to taper ... like the torpedo-shaped ends of a dog's pile of ... well, never mind.

We're talking about liberals in this book, so we absolutely must talk about Democrats. My paternal grandfather was born in 1897 and was a farmer in north Georgia. He also happened to be the Banks County tax collector in the mid-twentieth century. A Democrat. I don't know much about his views on politics, but I do know that the Democratic Party has changed since then. We need not go back fifty years. Just look at what they've become within the last few; a bunch of whining and vindictive brats. They need their little butts spanked! Of course, they would either enjoy that or denounce it as child abuse.

The only Democrats I've recently heard say anything that resembles common sense have been Joe Lieberman and Zell Miller. Senator Lieberman subsequently voted against Senator Isakson's common sense amendment to the Comprehensive Immigration Reform Act of 2006, so cross Lieberman off the page as well. There are probably a few others out there who make a little sense ... somewhere.

Mostly I see people like Ted Kennedy, John Kerry, Hillary Clinton, and a host of others who will say absolutely anything to elevate their own sense of control. They're like piranha feverishly rushing to feed upon the fatted thighs of lazy America for their sustenance. Are *you* feeding them?

The people who really drive me nuts are those who vote Democrat because they liked the way things were going sixty years ago or simply because that's the way their parents voted. They put no more thought into their decisions than that. Scary! Strict allegiance to a party rather than your own core values will find you looking at the TV one evening and shouting, "I've been supporting that clown?"

Approximately nine of ten candidates for whom I've voted in all elections have been Republicans. That's because I felt like those candidates best represented my ideals within the races they were running. That does *not* mean they would've been my first choices in every case or that they were truly the best people for the jobs. You really do feel a lot of the time like you're selecting the lesser of two or more evils. Helping to get your candidate elected also doesn't mean he or she will perform as expected once in office.

Other times evil is what people want. How else can you explain people actually voting for Ted Kennedy, who's been hiding under the leathery wing of pink Massachusetts for decades? How do you describe the people who elected Hillary Clinton to office in New York? One word, which may ironically be the root word of Massachusetts ... *masochistic.*

People who vote straight party tickets without thinking are the cattle of our nation. "Moooo! Must select Democrat. FDR was Democrat. Must pick Democrat. Government give me check. Moooo!" To slaughter we will go.

Candidates can be Democrats without being flaming liberals. Republicans can be criticized by their own for not being "right" enough. The overall game doesn't contain such clearly drawn lines as the concepts of good and evil, black and white, or right and wrong. What does provide a crystal clear line is the border between liberalism and Conservatism. There are those who might try to claim they ride the fence between the two. These are just the people who are trying to break free of their liberal backgrounds and enter greener pastures not fraught with leftist cow pies.

Look at the history of the Democratic Party during the latter part of the twentieth century. This is the party that salutes the Kennedy family as "American royalty."

American royalty? The Kennedy family is nothing but a criminal enterprise and dear Teddy is their CEO. Would John Kennedy have been assassinated had it not been for the family's ties to organized crime? Would Robert have been killed had it not been for the family's ties to organized crime before he pursued them as Attorney General?

So now we're left with the Chappaquiddick Chump. John had charisma. Robert had drive. Ted has a hangover. American royalty? Again consider Al Capone. He was a filthy-rich bootlegging criminal implicated in murders but convicted of none. He by the same standards deserves the label *American royalty* as much as any Kennedy.

Give these great books a try if you care to learn more about the so-called royal family:

Senatorial Privilege: The Chappaquiddick Cover-Up, by Leo Damore.

Double Cross, by Sam and Chuck Giancana.

Lloyd Bentsen meant to insult Dan Quayle in 1988 when during a debate he smugly said, "Senator, you're no Jack Kennedy." Senator Quayle was angered by the comment, but there are plenty of reasons to have taken the intended insult as a complement.

Of whom do you think when you ponder the phrase American royalty? Let me try that. Who's worthy of the title and not a criminal or liberal? I'm thinking of my parents. Now there's true royalty.

If I had to name American royalty within the political world I would immediately say Ronald and Nancy Reagan. A close second would be George H.W. and Barbara Bush. There may have been some Democratic couples worthy of this label, but if so then they were before my time. How could anyone not look upon Barbara Bush, Nancy Reagan, and Laura Bush and not see pure class? Compare any one of them to Hillary Clinton. You can't. There is no comparison. Just what we see in public is enough information to arrive at this conclusion. The differences can't be reduced to the labels Republican vs. Democrat, but rather the much more basic issues of good vs. evil.

I won't get into the intricacies of the Reagan presidency. There are plenty of other books that address those complex issues. I had the privilege of attending one of President Reagan's speeches in Atlanta. I missed one of my college math classes to attend the speech. I definitely made the correct decision. My math professor agreed.

Thank you, President Reagan, for your eight years of leadership and strength at what must be one of the most difficult jobs in the world. Rest in peace.

Now consider Jimmy Carter's recent abomination at the Coretta Scott King funeral when he took the opportunity to whine about wiretapping procedures of the Bush administration. There's no way that Ronald Reagan would've ever tried to turn a funeral into a forum of political commentary to denounce anyone, especially a current President ... a current President who also happened to be attending the same funeral!

Shame on you, Jimmy Carter, for that unforgivable outrage. Shame on you for the way you mishandled your presidency and for leaving your political waste for President Reagan to flush. Shame on you for embarrassing the state of Georgia. Thank you for helping to keep the line between Conservatives and liberals crystal clear.

Shame on you, Bill Clinton, for leaving your political waste for President George W. Bush to flush. Shame on you for reducing the White House to the Whore House. You were the perfect liberal politician ... a perpetrator of that which is vile.

Many Americans (primarily liberals) have forgotten 9/11. They've forgotten what it felt like to watch the towers fall. I turned on my TV that morning and watched live as the second plane impacted the second tower. I'll never forget or forgive that. Why do so many liberal Democrats seem to have done both?

Many Americans are feeling that if you're not for us, then you're against us. I'm one of them. That statement is directed to our politicians as much as to Osama bin Laden and his company of sand devils. The same statement goes for our citizens who continue to speak venomously against the United States. The statement goes for the country of France. The statement goes for Mexico.

Democrats and many Republicans alike have been ignoring the voice of the American people. We want the damned borders sealed! We want the FairTax! We want social security overhauled if not privatized, and we want welfare greatly reduced!

I'm not alone in declaring my disgust for former Senator Tom Daschle of South Dakota. He stood with members of Congress singing *God Bless America* following the 9/11 attacks. There was a tremendous feeling of American oneness at that time. The country pulled together despite race, political affiliation, or geographical location. The entire country was behind New York. Democrats had their little show of mourning, but soon returned to business as usual. For Daschle and company that meant hammering President Bush and trying to work any greasy angle they could to concoct political gain. How could anyone have watched that occur and still vote Democrat? I whittle away the short list of possible reasons and am left with only two. Corruption or stupidity. Maybe both.

The disease of liberalism seemed to be in remission within the Democratic Party as the dust of 9/11 settled around them. They seemed almost like responsible adults. They almost seemed like they loved this country. They almost seemed like they for once weren't possessed within the hellish claws of left wing control.

Don't take my word for it now. We have the Internet ... thanks to Al Gore. Run a search of the comments in the news following 9/11. Investigate the likes of Tom Daschle, John Kerry, and Dianne Feinstein. Read what they said in 2001 and compare that to their comments and behavior today.

"Bush lied!" they scream.

Yeah, that's what happened. President Bush made up 9/11 and the circumstances surrounding it. I see it all so clearly now. The Democrats aren't the liars. Bush lied. The disappearance of the twin towers was really just a big magic trick. No plane hit the Pentagon. No plane crashed in Pennsylvania after American heroes thwarted the targeting of the White House. Everything the President has done since 9/11 to combat terrorism has been a huge façade to prolong the magic trick. Thousands of people didn't really die. Bush orchestrated all of this according to liberals, while in the same breath they accuse him of being unintelligent. Well, which is it, pink party?

Saddam Hussein was really our good friend. The wiretaps haven't been for the purpose of defeating terrorism. Those evil Conservatives are actually trying to listen in as women call their husbands to pick up bread and milk on their way home from work. You liberals caught them red-handed! The right really wants to know where you keep your marijuana stashes and what you've been doing with your law office interns. None of the information relates to tracking the activity of those wonderful Middle Easterners who just want to kill your children. Bush lied indeed! The left's good friend Osama bin Laden is the one who's been telling the truth from the start. How could we have been so blind?

Democrats just couldn't stomach the thought of supporting a Republican regime in defense of our nation. They were willing to cast aside the suffering of 9/11 victims and their families soon after the attack and conduct attacks of their own for the sole purpose of trying to gain political power. They can't have a Republican President look good by defeating the terrorists who perpetrated 9/11. What they have to do is try to undermine the man and convince the voting cattle of America to look for the D's rather than the R's on future ballots.

Power is a monstrous corrupter. Everyone wants power. Liberal Democrats don't have it and are simply willing to do absolutely anything to acquire it. How ironic it is that these same liberals are the ones secondarily responsible for 9/11, in line directly on the heels of their good friend Osama.

How do we explain the post-9/11 behavior of liberal Democrats? Everyone can present their own theories. One might be that they felt guilty about their years of pandering and weak-handedness with regard to the terrorists with whom we're at war. That's giving Democrats a lot of credit. One must assume that a conscience has to be in place in order to feel guilt. I find that possibility doubtful in their case. I'll stick with my theory that they want the power.

There is at least some hope for the voters who are too stupid to realize these things about politicians. As for those who are part of the corruption, there's a line in the sand you love and you're on the other side of it. The Democratic Party has become a safehaven for terrorists.

Not so fast, Republicans! You don't deserve to go unscathed. Many of you haven't been listening to those of us who put you into office. Consider the words of Bill Cosby:

"You know, I brought you in this world. I can take you out."[6]

Mr. Cosby was of course making a joke about his children during a stand-up comedy routine, and funny it was. I'm not talking about "taking out" our politicians in the sense that John Kennedy experienced. I'm talking about ridding ourselves of them in the voting booths.

I sincerely believe that people have been so diluted and pumped full of false information and propaganda that they're literally too stupid to vote. There should be a competency exam to qualify to vote. Wow! Did you feel that wind? That was every Democrat in the US gasping. The modern representative party of the lazy and ignorant would scratch and pull hair over that proposition. So what? Bring it on.

Some Republicans actually voted "nay" on Senator Johnny Isakson's proposed amendment to immediately seal the southern border, as did Ted Kennedy. Anything that Ted Kennedy wants is typically either bad for America, good for Ted, or both. Everyone who voted "nay" on that amendment voted "nay" on America! Such behavior is expected of Democrats, but most of us expect better from Republicans. Tides have turned.

The majority of Americans want the southern border closed to illegal entry YESTERDAY! The amendment was nevertheless shot down by the Senate by a vote of 55-40! Eighteen of the 55 were Republicans and here they are, stripped naked for all of you to see:

Bennett (UT)   Lugar (IN)

Brownback (KS)   Martinez (FL)

Chafee (RI)	Murkowski (AK)
Coleman (MN)	Shelby (AL)
Collins (ME)	Snowe (ME)
Craig (ID)	Specter (PA)
DeWine (OH)	Stevens (AK)
Graham (SC)	Voinovich (OH)
Hagel (NE)	Warner (VA)

Four of the five who didn't vote at all were Republicans and one of the "nays" was a New England area Independent.[7] Who should stay and who should go? The power is yours if you live in any of these states and are registered to vote. Get rid of the dead weight and plug in someone who will better represent the needs of our country rather than the corruption of political shenanigans. I'm sure these senators have all kinds of well-rehearsed and colorful answers for why they violated out trust. Don't let them snow you. Every one of them has some underlying reason or reasons and none of them are in America's best interest. Trails of truth about why senators from any party would've voted "nay" to seal the border will all lead to power or money.

I voted for President George W. Bush. I have two "W" stickers on my vehicle. I don't know him. I've never met him. I do think that he's a good man based on what I've seen, heard, and read. I don't agree with everything his administration has done, but I shudder when I imagine what things would be like right now had John Kerry been elected in 2004 or Al Gore in 2000. We would probably all be wearing sandals and galabiyyas by now, and babbling some forked-tongue sand devil language.

President Bush has had to endure so much ridiculous fodder from the left that Conservatives are losing their patience with all Democrats, not just the radical nut-jobs. The concepts of free speech and the right to assemble have been pushed to the brink of criminal activity and treason. Disagreeing is one thing. Making harsh comments against our President and the United States during a time of war is the act of an enemy. Simply put, liberals *are* enemies of the United States of America.

President Bush was correct to authorize military actions in the Middle East. That's a no-brainer, and being a no-brainer explains why it's so difficult for Democrats to comprehend. The part of the war against terroristic Islam I'm not happy about is that I would like to have seen the enemy hit much harder. I'm no military strategist, but I like a firearm with a lot of recoil. Osama likes big explosions? I say give him and his kind what they want.

The President has stood firm on our need to use wiretapping and other techniques to collect information on the terrorism we're battling. Another no-brainer. I personally don't care if the NSA listens to every single phone call I make. I'm actually amazed that people think they really have that desire or capability. Do you lefties actually believe the NSA gives a crap about the private phone calls of America's average citizens? I still say you're terrified they will find out about your drug stashes and what you've been doing with your law office interns! Such intense concern for our rights should be concentrated on radically reforming our taxation and social security systems instead of whining about phone call recordings.

The areas in which I'm not pleased with the Bush administration have been government spending and immigration. You're an idiot if you thought I was going to say gas prices.

Government spending is occurring at a rate as badly as if John Kerry or Al Gore *had* been elected and that's despicable. Much of the problem has been the current regime's mimicking of the Democratic tactic of pandering to the lazy and stupid voters. *Moooo!*

Fishing for potential voters is why the Bush administration has continuously dropped the ball on the issue of illegal aliens. This also mimicked the irresponsibility and self-serving aspects of Democrats.

I'm a legal citizen and voter in this country and I'm part of the majority that demands the sealing of the Mexican border. No more illegals! Not one! Once *all* our borders are secure, then we can decide who stays and who gets arrested and deported.

We're told that Mexico is our friend and yet we see Mexicans waving the Mexican flag within US cities, flying the US flag upside down, and speaking anti-American rhetoric. We hear Mexico threatening to sue our country. We hear of border agents being shot at along the border. Illegals come here to work and then send *our* money to Mexico.

These are hostile acts against our security and economy. Democrats and Republicans alike are too greedy to say so. There's a way to handle the problem. We issue a military warning that anyone crossing our borders illegally may be shot. The next step is to follow through when necessary and show that the warning hadn't just been an empty threat. Very little ammunition would be required to seal our borders under those circumstances. This isn't a very large planet anymore and we have quite enough people in this country now. Legal arrivals are welcome and all others aren't. I'm still partial to my fifty-first state idea, though.

Our political officials from both sides (the asses and the elephants) had better start listening to us quickly or else getting voted from office will be the least of their worries. How they will react to the explosive civil war that's brewing in America right now will suddenly become agenda item *numero uno*.

I still think that President Bush has done a decent job considering what he's had to work with. The man is trying to juggle a war along with so many other pressing issues and every step of the way he encounters disgraceful leftist gasbags obstructing him. I frankly don't know why any sane person would want the job of President anymore. I'd like to think that the reason would be the same as for those of us who want to be police officers or soldiers. Not for what the position can do for you and your interests, but purely because of a sense of American duty. If that were the case with our so-called leaders, then it wouldn't make much of a difference with what party they were affiliated.

A huge difference between Democrats and Republicans that I've noticed in recent years has been the way they voice their opinions of one another. Liberal Democrats stoop to childish name-calling in debates, because they have no solid base and become frustrated. Who can forget the on-air battle between Sean Hannity and Alec Baldwin? I'm sure Alec would like to forget it. That was like a cat playing with a mouse. There was name-calling from both camps, but that was the extent of Alec's argument. He had nothing more in his arsenal than phrases like "no-talent whore" and "cabin boy." Sean called him on his reckless and unfounded political statements and poor Alec had a meltdown. Alec was just upset because he dirtied his big pink diaper. They cleaned him up and after a while he was able to return to the depths of Hollywood obscurity from whence he came. [8]

Democrats regularly resort to childish antics. The fact that they even still have a party is indicative of the number of brain-dead people lumbering to the poles like zombies. The favorite word of liberal Democrats is "Nazi." Anyone with whom they disagree suddenly becomes a "racist" or a "Nazi." This is just evidence once again of their lack of moral and political base. They're worse than angry kids kicking sand at their teachers on a playground.

Many people are wondering what exactly is the agenda of most Democrats. The only clear consistency across their party is that they want everything given to them for free. If there is any real common thread, then that's it. One other relatively consistent trait is that with few exceptions the Democrats are embarrassments to themselves and the United States. More and more so-called Republicans are unfortunately following suit.

Have you ever wondered how anyone could switch parties if their beliefs in what they're doing are strong, given the differences between Republicans and Democrats? I have. I realize that there are a lot of factors in the mix of politics that could effect such a decision, but flip-flopping between parties can occur just as readily as flip-flopping on issues. Whatever you want to hear is what they will say. Whatever you want them to do is what they say they will do. God save you if you take them all at their word. Party switching occurs because politicians seek the path of least resistance to power. Screw the affiliation and anyone who gets in their way.

The Democratic Party has become one of extreme negativity in the twenty-first century. This isn't to suggest that Republicans have been 100% better, but Democrats have been absolutely laughable. They seem utterly incapable of pro-ducing any positive work. The majority of their waking hours have been dedi-cated to searching for ways to adamantly and without cause oppose anything proposed by Republicans. Two primary things have resulted from this. One is that our politicians are getting nothing done because of their tug-of-war contests. The other result is that we as the American people are suffering the consequences.

Enemies of the United States are at work within every level of government as we speak. Sounds bleak, huh? So what do we do about it? The voting cattle cast their uneducated and biased ballots caring about nothing beyond R's and D's. They even factor in candidates' race, gender, physical appearance, and which ones have the snappiest TV ads and campaign signs! The cattle are stupid and biased. We've been through all that. The question is how do we fix these prob-lems?

I personally would love to see a third party draw some serious backing. Inde-pendent and Libertarian Parties try, but they never seem to make much of a dent. Well someone other than the R's and D's deserves a chance to serve without greed as the main ingredient of their platform.

I'd really like to see the appearance of a brand new party. I envision an entity that's dedicated to returning to the core ideals upon which this country was built. Just 230 years ago we had to convince our good friends the British that the United States was serious about "moving out of the house." That story was best explained not by any college professor, but by Andy Taylor to his son Opie in an episode of the greatest television show ever made.[9] Sorry, but neither *American Idol* nor *Survivor* qualify. I'm referring to *The Andy Griffith Show*. The episode was called "Andy Discovers America." Check it out if you've never seen it, because it was one of the many classics of the series.

Let's build a hypothetical new party right now. We could call this new party the American Party. All thoughts and opinions would be welcome, even the warm and fuzzy right-brained ideas of the leftists. They do have their place. Decisions would ultimately be dictated by common sense, though. How wonderful would that be? There would be no place at all reserved for the lazy welfare crowd or self-serving special interest groups. They would have to either shape up or fade into extinction. Diplomacy would be welcome and preferred, but never used as a replacement for a necessary military action. Force would be employed when and if talking failed. Try to negotiate first and if that fails then we shoot, and when we need to shoot we don't hesitate.

In other words, carry a big gun and a demeanor of authority and there will probably not be a need to shoot. I'm thinking of a terrific line from the movie *The Karate Kid*:

Mr. Miyagi was quizzing Daniel-son on why he felt he needed to learn karate. The boy told his teacher he wanted to learn karate so he'd know how to fight. Seeing disappointment in Mr. Miyagi's eyes, Daniel-son considered his response a few moments and changed it to, "So I won't have to fight." Mr. Miyagi was pleased and Daniel-son realized that was the answer the teacher sought.[10]

A fictional boy figured out the correct answer to the question about why he needed to be able to defend himself. Isn't it a shame that liberal Democrats in real life can't translate the same understanding to our country? Neither Conservatives nor liberals *want* to go into battle. The difference is that at least Conservatives are willing to go when necessary. There is one type that does enjoy fighting. When they're kids we call them bullies. When they're grown we call them terrorists.

The American Party would stand for Americans and Americans *only*. That would include people who are already legal citizens of this country and anyone wishing to legally immigrate and become citizens. Illegal aliens would be treated like the criminals they are, each and every one a potential threat to our national security and a definite threat to our economic system.

The national language would be English and those expecting to come here for anything other than a holiday tour had better learn the language and learn to read and write it properly. I had to pass college English, where one misspelled word or other infraction within a formal composition was an automatic F. Why should the standards be much less for people immigrating to the US?

The American Party would encourage free trade with just enough regulations to monitor for criminal activity.

They would seek to eliminate racism and bigotry in their traditional forms and in their modern forms, such as affirmative action, the NAACP, the ACLU, etcetera. Another unnecessary entity would be unions. Like affirmative action, unions once had a purpose and any legitimate need for them has ended.

Social security would be discontinued. People should be allowed to invest their money on their own or blow it as they see fit. That would be the peoples' business, not that of the federal government. Those who had paid into social security would receive immediate refunds based on a prorated amount of how much they had paid to date. Those who had never worked would have to start. An investigation would need to be conducted to see if any of our current politicians or former ones still alive should be prosecuted for fraud on the handling of the abolished social security system.

Those wishing to donate money toward a welfare bank to help support those incapable of caring for themselves would receive such opportunity. Those not wanting to donate would have none of their taxes directed to the program. Listen up, you lazy members of the welfare class who *used* to get government checks in the mail. That's over!

American Party representatives would push to operate under a national sales tax. The income tax code would be hauled to the Smithsonian on a flatbed truck and placed on display. Everyone could look at the stacks of paper and laugh at how idiotic people could be when they set their minds to the task. Oh, and most of you weak links formerly called "the poor" get a new and longer title: the "Self-Hurting Income Troubled." Maybe we'll discuss your acronym in a future book.

We would need some changes to our laws, such as how about we start enforcing them with great fury? The only new law we would really need to put on the already overloaded books would be "dereliction of parental duty," which would of course be a felony.

The American Party would have strong leadership from top to bottom. All energies would be directed to accomplishing positive things for the country. That would mean we would need a new branch of news media if positive things were to be reported, especially if we also were to expect truth and lack of bias.

Who would be our presidential candidate? Whew! That's a tough one. I nominate Herman Cain.

I'd like to think that all of this would work. This *would* work if we started a new country somewhere. Maybe Atlantis will resurface, because our chances of such a Utopian society are slim here unless we can send Katrina-the-hit-woman to the home of every politically motivated liberal in the nation.

The conclusion to all this is that Republicans have begun to let us down and Democrats are maintaining their tradition of doing so. The best Democrats can offer is "Bush lied." Well, somebody lied and it wasn't President Bush. The liberal media and liberal Democrats lied! Ask the men and women of our armed forces who have served in Iraq who lied, and who continues to do so. As a matter of fact, let's ask the Iraqi people themselves. You're a lot less likely to hear "Bush lied" from them as you are to hear, "Thank you, President Bush!"

Democrat … Republican … who cares anymore? We've seen a multitude of examples proving that people need not be Conservatives to be Republicans, or liberals to be Democrats. Core America needs a new representative body that leaves the others wallowing in their corruption and red tape, but sleeping America seems more concerned with Xbox 360 and the prophetic arrival of the next PlayStation. Our only hope right now really does seem to lie within the slim chance that we can start our own country, if and when a new land mass appears. Oh, hell, we just might need our own planet!

9

LIBERALS IN ACTION

Now let's expose liberal behavior in real life situations. The world can be our test laboratory and liberals will be our lab rats. How fitting. There's no better way to present the faults of a particular manner of thought than by pointing out the resulting behavior.

We've all watched violent Islam's behavior. We have baseball and apple pie. They have car bombs and the Koran. We've watched Congresswoman Cynthia McKinney represent her district and her state with the childish antics of an undisciplined six-year-old. Speaking of her again, I just saw a separated-at-birth comparison between Cynthia McKinney in one of her many wild-eyed moments and Buckwheat.[11] I must say that I was appalled and offended by that image! Poor taste!

Buckwheat was one of my favorite TV personalities of childhood. There's no comparison between Georgia's 4th District incompetent and that cute little kid from *The Little Rascals*. Mr. Wheat's (Billie Thomas) family should complain.

We watched Michael Moore have a characteristic moment of verbal flatulence at the 2003 Oscars with his "shame on you" acceptance speech. A loser with a camera will never be anything more than a loser with a camera.

We've seen Cindy Sheehan disgrace herself, her family, her country, and especially her son repeatedly since he was killed in Iraq in 2004. The liberal media has been more than willing to let this one have plenty of air time. Cindy, what would Casey have to say about your being a traitor and palling about with communist dictators? First we had Hanoi Jane. Now we've got Hugo-huggin' Cindy.

I mentioned Georgia embarrassment Jimmy Carter using the Coretta Scott King funeral as a liberal political forum. Let us not leave out the good Reverend Joseph Lowery. A funeral is a religious event, a chance to mourn and honor the deceased, to provide closure for the bereaved family. The event might even be considered a celebration in some cases. What a funeral isn't is an opportunity to express political opinion. If Coretta King would've approved of what Lowery and

Carter did, then she's not the woman we're told she was. The same for her husband. Hey, Joe. God's still mad at you, but Satan sends his warmest regards.

We were informed that in May of 2006 the FBI executed a search warrant at the office and home of Louisiana Democrat William Jefferson after he accepted a $100,000.00 cash bribe.[12] People across the country should be outraged at Jefferson and thankful for law enforcement's work on the matter. This goes for politicians and the public alike, regardless of party affiliations. What reaction do we observe from our elected officials, though? We see Republicans and Democrats alike screaming in opposition to the FBI's actions. Only a criminal would seek to shroud criminal behavior and try to redirect the focus of the story. The only conclusions to be drawn from such behavior are that these elected officials really do see themselves as above the law, and perhaps more search warrants would lead to other freezers full of more than just T-bones. Wake up, America! These are the types of people you elect and re-elect.

Bill Clinton took us to be a country of idiots when he proudly declared "I didn't inhale" and "I did not have sexual relations with that woman ... not one time." He was about half correct on both accounts.

We all got to watch the Dixie Chicks chop off their own heads when the lead singer publicly denounced President George W. Bush in London. Denouncing a Republican US President during war-time has become the number one liberal pastime, but that's probably not the smartest thing to do when you're a country singer and your fan-base is predominantly Conservative. Free speech can be quite expensive when disconnected from good sense, huh Miss Maines? Go *make nice* with the pop culture, because you burned your bridge to country. Will you be ready to *make nice* right before a plane your on explodes or slams into a building?

Liberals like to burn things. The US flag makes for their favorite barbecue, but they will settle for books, clothing, or anything else with which they can concoct issues. Too bad they don't put the clothes on prior to torching them. You can't repeatedly play with fire and not eventually get hurt or hurt someone else. That's never been much of a liberal concern, but why light up when you can launch away? Yes, I much prefer throwing things over burning them. I've found that a Sheryl Crow or Pretenders CD will fly up to sixty yards if you launch them at the correct angle. You only get one throw, because the things fly apart like the liberal thought process.

We've been victimized by some absolutely asinine comments from the left. I'm talking about comments that were so nutty that they seem to have originated from the posteriors of these people rather than whatever semblance of a brain they claim to possess. There's no sense in repeating their idiotic statements here.

They've been exposed before like the chunky stuff at the water treatment plant. Just log onto the Web and run some searches for the moronic things that have been emitted from one orifice or another from the following:

Ed Asner (often spelled with two S's), Susan Sarandon, Oliver Stone, Robin Williams, Tim Robbins, Sean Penn, Spike Lee, Jessica Lange, Jane Fonda, Janeane Garofalo, Dave Matthews, Chevy Chase, Bill Maher, and Avril Lavigne (I'd really like to see what she looks like cleaned up, though). How about Harry Belafonte? Who dug up that obscure old relic? Hey, Harry, your *day-o* was a long time ago. I'm not sure it was even fifteen minutes.

Hillary Clinton regularly sticks her foot into her mouth and I can't begin to imagine what that must taste like. I'm thinking molded French cheese. Oh, and who can forget Madonna? Well, I did. Women who sell sex for money are called prostitutes downtown. Liberals call them entertainers.

The list goes on. These people and their left wing support group regularly do and say such odd things that it's difficult to tell what's normal and what's not anymore when you look to the left horizon.

So much for the more famous liberals in action. Let's now take a more focused look under the liberal microscope and examine some localized liberals in action. These are true incidents from around my home in Georgia. Some of these liberal sightings were relayed to me by others who witnessed them firsthand. Screw you, counselor. Hearsay is allowed in this book.

Some of these liberal sightings occurred while I was on the job as a law enforcement officer. Liberals have quite regular run-ins with the law, so that source of material wasn't to be avoided. Laws after all do not apply to liberals, aside from those addressing ecological issues. Such thinking leads to behavior that tends to attract the attention of the fine men and women of American law enforcement. Am I suggesting that most criminals are liberals? Uhmm … yes, pretty much.

LIBERAL SIGHTING #1:

Allow me to take you back to July 17, 1994. I'd been a police officer for a year and a half and had spent that time working evening shift in a very criminally active area of the county. Before I worked this area I'd been told that if the county ever received an enema, then the tube would be inserted here. Whoever told me that had been correct.

The time was 2109 hours. That's 9:09 p.m. for you liberals. I responded to a dispatch at a house from where a man named Mark had called and requested to be arrested. Excellent, I thought. We aim to serve.

I arrived at the house cautiously for obvious reasons and saw a white male seated upon the front steps beneath the porch light. He saw me approach, stood up, and opened the front door releasing two large dogs to roam the front yard. I didn't exit my cruiser at that time, because my options were to, (a) hope the dogs weren't vicious and take that chance, (b) have to shoot the dogs if I lost that bet.

My door was open enough for me to hear the man say to his wife inside, "The police are here. Get the video camera."

Her reply was, "Mark, stop it. Get the dogs back in here."

The dogs returned to the interior of the house and the door was closed. My back-up arrived and the two of us met the "man" and his wife at the midpoint of the driveway.

I asked Mark what he wanted and he was immediately confrontational. "Do you have a warrant to be here?" he asked.

"We don't need one. What can we do for you?"

"Don't you need a warrant to be here?" Mark repeated.

"Is there something we can help you with or not? You're the one who called us."

Mark gave me his full name and date of birth when I requested the information. He became argumentative with the back-up officer about why we were there as I ran an NCIC check on him. His words were slurred and he stank of alcoholic beverages and liberalism.

Mark decided this would be a good time to go back inside his home, which I wasn't going to allow because of the dogs on the opposite side of the front door. I ordered him to stop several times and he refused, so I got to him before he got to his front door and I arrested him.

I asked Mark's intoxicated wife Betty why he'd done this.

"We're from the north," Betty replied, like this should make perfect sense to me. In some ways it did.

"What?"

"He did this to prove a point," she added. "He was recently arrested for domestic violence and was trying to prove a point."

That at least explained why Betty was on crutches, but her answer didn't really satisfy my question. Perhaps someone from the north could explain this to me.

Mark was transported to the county jail and charged with obstruction and reckless conduct. He became belligerent at the jail and began banging his head against a window. I was willing to let him continue banging his head because it would've been the most constructive thing he'd done with it all evening, but the intake deputies were having none of that. Mark had one foot in the padded cell for *special guests* as I departed. The other one was still stuck in his mouth.

Mark defended himself in a jury trial in February of 1995, so naturally he was convicted of both counts. You know the old saying; any man who defends himself has a liberal for a client.

LIBERAL SIGHTING #2:

The war on Christmas waged by liberals struck close to home in December of 2005. I was walking my then seven-year-old daughter home from school one afternoon and our conversation went something like this:

"Daddy, guess what we get to do at school tomorrow."

"I don't know. What do you get to do?"

"We get to have a party."

"Oh, a Christmas party. Fun."

"Yeah, only we can't call it a Christmas party. We have to just call it a party."

Anger already began to rise within me, because I knew what was coming next. I'd heard and seen many of the reports of liberals using their hearings and court proceedings to try to eliminate God from our lives. At that moment I began to give some serious thought to removing my little girl from the government school system and placing her in a private school, or perhaps home-schooling her.

"Why can't you call it a Christmas party?" I asked as calmly as possible through clenched teeth.

"Because not everybody has Christmas."

"That's true," I told her, "but we do and we still will. You have my permission to call your party a Christmas party at home *and* at school. Let me know if you get into trouble about saying the word Christmas and I'll take care of it."

My daughter is a very passive and thoughtful little girl. She looked at me with her large blue eyes and then looked away.

"Okay?" I pressed.

"Okay."

"We called our holiday Christmas long before these people came along who want to get rid of the word. We're not changing for them. You're having a *Christmas* party tomorrow."

The point I continued making to my daughter was that if someone says "happy Hanukkah," that was fine, or "Merry Christmas," or even the dreaded "happy holidays." What we will not do is alter our lifestyles in any way to accommodate non-believers trying to impose their theories upon us.

Isn't it amazing how such otherwise mystical thinkers as liberals refuse to acknowledge God? My personal theory about them is that they really are believers. Most of them just happen to be on the opposing team. I haven't been attending church regularly. I'm no expert on the Bible and I certainly don't walk around quoting scriptures, but there's one piece that always stayed in the forefront of memory because of its relevance to this life in general:

II Corinthians, 11:14

And no marvel, for Satan himself is transformed into an angel of light.

Don't get your drawers in a wad. I'm not suggesting that liberals are all evil. They just get the worst possible results from the best of intentions sometimes.

I'm also not suggesting that all Conservatives are Godly people. Their avenues of getting from intentions to results can sometimes get them into trouble.

Where do all these struggles leave us regarding good and evil, Conservative and liberal? I don't have all the answers anymore than anyone else, but I do know this much. If liberals want to find out how far I'm willing to go to defend my beliefs, then keep trying to infiltrate my little girl's thinking.

In the meantime ... Merry Christmas!

LIBERAL SIGHTING #3:

Today I saw a liberal. I knew she was afflicted with the disease and she didn't have to say a word. No, it wasn't the faded Kerry-Edwards sticker. I couldn't see that until she drove away, because the bicycle rack on her car concealed it and the license plate.

The reason I knew this woman was a liberal was because she loaded her groceries into her car and then released the shopping cart. She watched it roll across the lot and turned her back before it crashed into the side of a Mercedes SUV. At least she had enough of a trace of conscience not to want to behold the destructivity of her work. I guess that's a grazing liberal instead of a meat eater.

LIBERAL SIGHTING #4:

In late 1993 I responded to a domestic dispute between a mother and son. A police officer never knows exactly what's happening on domestic calls and they're definitely amongst the most dangerous. This particular mother called 911 not because her twelve-year-old son was uncontrollable or was attacking her. He hadn't destroyed property or even cussed her out. She'd called the police because he wouldn't wash the dishes.

LIBERAL SIGHTING #5:

Sometimes you can hear liberals coming before you even see them. They don't have to speak. These sightings are not rare and can be experienced by anyone outside rural America.

Liberals like to impose upon you with their wacky ideas, their cigarette smoke, etcetera, but what I'm getting to here is that they thoroughly enjoy imposing their "music" upon you. Listen for the *thump-thump-thump* and the rattling of car parts around urban intersections. The noise is commonly laced with foul language, violence, and racist ideology. The liberal occupants sit low in the seats and low in society, both by choice. This is the soundtrack of liberal America.

LIBERAL SIGHTING #6:

A fourteen-year-old liberal had been living with his mother and giving her fits, so the parents decided the boy should live with dad for a while.

Dad and son had a heated argument one afternoon and the boy called 911. I responded and listened to both sides. The boy was a defiant smart-ass and said his father had struck him. The boy informed me it was illegal for anyone to strike another person. This kid had about seven years of behavioral delay going on, but I can't actually blame mom for that since I'd never met her and didn't know enough of the details.

I talked with the boy's father at length. He said he was trying to instill some discipline into his son before it was too late. He'd indeed spanked the boy with a belt for back-talking and other infractions. He understood that fourteen was a bit older than usual to begin issuing spankings, but better late than never. His concern was that the boy had threatened to call the police to report child abuse if he spanked him. He'd called his son's bluff and spanked him anyway. The boy had made good on his threat, which had been what brought me to their apartment.

I privately explained to dad that his use of the belt didn't qualify as assault under Georgia law as long as he didn't go overboard. State law appropriately states that neither simple assault nor simple battery apply to parents administering "corporal punishment" to their children.

Things were relatively calm when I left the apartment, but it wasn't long before I was right back there again. Dad had spanked the boy again because of more sass. The boy informed me that his father had struck him with a belt and he wanted him arrested.

"Are you bleeding?" I asked the boy.

"No!"

"Are you injured?"

"No!"

"Do you have marks? You were spanked with a belt through blue jeans. Are you able to sit down?"

"Huh?"

"My father always warned me the last time before a spanking that I 'wouldn't be able to sit down for a week' if I didn't stop whatever I was doing to draw his wrath. Are you able to sit down?"

"Yes, but he beat me and I want him arrested!"

I turned to the boy's father. "Sir, you had better show me exactly what you did. I need to document whether or not child abuse has occurred here."

Dad looked at me in disbelief that lasted only a moment. He then masterfully extracted his belt from the loops of his pants with a single fluid motion. He looked like Bruce Lee wielding a pair of nunchakus as he closed upon his wide-eyed son. Every lick was on target in and around the bull's-eye of junior's backside.

"No sir," I said to dad when he'd finished the boy's third spanking of the day. "That doesn't qualify as child abuse."

I left the apartment, documented the incidents in detail in my police report, and didn't get any further calls to that apartment.

LIBERAL SIGHTING #7:

A woman felt sorry for a homeless man on Highway 41 north of Atlanta at the same time she needed some work done at her house. The work wasn't difficult. Just the removal of some trash.

The woman stopped and offered the man the simple job, which he gladly accepted. Being homeless and jobless, naturally he was chomping at the bit to acquire gainful employment.

She drove him to her home. There he experienced an instantaneous changing of the mind and decided he really didn't want to work. He just wanted lunch.

The woman refused and told the man to leave. He did, but not before scratching her car in retaliation. My question to you is, which one was the liberal?

You are correct.

LIBERAL SIGHTING #8:

Bears are Conservatives. Liberals don't know this. Liberals in national parks think they can tame the creatures the same way they believe they can control

Conservatives in politics. Lefties in both situations wind up getting mauled, chewed up, and spit out.

Parks have rules, but those don't apply to the left as has already been noted. In the fall of 2005 my wife and I were traveling along a gravel road near the Grand Tetons in Wyoming. Several vehicles had stopped alongside the road, so we stopped to find out what the attraction was.

A couple of black bear cubs were lingering within a marshy area between the woods and road. Terrific. A great sighting, but the mother was sitting in shallow water about ten feet from the edge of the road eating something from the limbs of the bushes.

A camera-toting lib headed toward her. We went the other way. The last time I looked back this guy was about twenty feet from the Conservative quadruped and inching closer. Something told me that it wasn't a real good idea to be closer to mama bear than to our car. Perhaps it was common sense.

We left before we found out whether or not the bear had New England ham to go with her berries.

LIBERAL SIGHTING #9:

Liberals are *always* innocent. A lefty could be facing a mountain of evidence including videotape, DNA, fingerprints, and a host of witnesses, but as long as he's guilty he'll maintain that he's not. Every good sociopath must learn to lie if he's to promote his cause. He must be able and willing to convincingly deny the very nose on his face. Every good liberal must also teach his children to do the same.

I went on a series of three search warrants executed by the two detectives I supervised. They had been analyzing burglaries that had been occurring almost daily in the area of a local high school. They had figured out who was probably doing the burglaries using crime analysis procedures.

Several fine young liberals had been skipping school on some of the dates that just happened to coincide with the incidents. They became the targets of surveillance by the two detectives.

One lovely morning in late May of 2006 the government's "No Thug Left Behind" program saw to it that the young thuglets again found their way onto the campus of a high school within a district they didn't reside. They decided that this day would be a good one to use for burglaries rather than learning to properly read and write English, so they headed off campus, only this time they were masterfully followed.

The detectives observed them remove a window screen from a house and attempt entry. Uniform units were called into the area. A marked cruiser pulled into the driveway of the would-be burglary victim's home and thuglets scattered like a covey of quail. Too bad the police dogs weren't present.

The teens were all captured and placed into the county youth detention facility, which means even less than it does to go to jail. Either one might as well be a hotel utilized at taxpayer expense, room service included.

The detectives obtained search warrants for the homes of all three thuglets to try to recover the thousands of dollars worth of stolen property from prior burglaries. I arrived at work at about that time and was informed of what had occurred, so I went along for the execution of the search warrants.

The first house to which we went was occupied by the primary thuglet's father and younger siblings. I entered the living room as a detective was explaining the day's events to the father, who was testing the support capability of a recliner after his long hard day of doing whatever. My first thought was that he looked like a combination of Buddha and Racial Ray Nagin.

"Couldn't have been my son," I heard Buddha tell the detective.

"Couldn't have been your son? Well, I regret to inform you that it *was* your son."

"Couldn't have been."

"Sir, we already had him as a suspect before today. He'd been skipping school. We followed him off campus today and watched him trying to break into a house. What part of that are you having difficulty understanding?"

"Well, it might have been him today, but he couldn't have done any of those other burglaries. He was in school."

"You mean like he was in school today?"

This is the kind of thing you encounter when trying to reason truth with a liberal. They want to pick apart the truth and anything that can't be proven with 100% surety just didn't happen, especially when it will cost them money for restitution.

Cash from one of the burglaries was recovered from a hole in the back of Buddha Nagin's couch, right where the one of the three thuglets who talked said it would be. The fact that one of them was cooperative with police showed that he wasn't too far gone to someday be saved from the jaws of liberalism. The other two will possibly be in your house someday while you're at work, stealing the things you went to work to pay for.

The detectives on this case discovered something very telling about liberals and the government school system. School records sometimes showed the thuglets present when it was proven they had been out doing burglaries. Great system, huh?

One other bit of information is worth mentioning regarding Buddha's home. The whole place stank like a giant litter box and none of us ever saw any animals with more than two legs. Saying that the family didn't flush might have been relevant not only in the figurative sense, but also the literal one.

LIBERAL SIGHTING #10:

Liberals in early 2006 sprang from their holes with a cheerful fervor unseen from them since 09-12-01. Vice President Dick Cheney was hunting birds with friends in Texas when he accidentally injured one of those friends with a load of bird-shot. End of story.

That wasn't the end of the story as far as the left was concerned, though. They painted daily pictures in the news that depicted the Vice President like a madman who had donned himself in facial paint, crept through the woods with an assault rifle, and hidden in a foxhole until the precise moment he could leap forward and unload upon unsuspecting human prey.

Liberals wanted Cheney charged. They screamed for his resignation. They received neither. The country had so many relevant issues in question at that time and the media chose to beat this story until there was nothing left but fur and eyeballs. There were more negative articles and cartoons about the Vice President during one month than there have been about their good buddy Osama in five years. In the end it was the media that was made to look ridiculous and at its own hand. They were the madmen waiting to pounce from their foxholes. They sprang forth with their pencils and microphones and blew off their own feet.

LIBERAL SIGHTING #11:

Several years ago I saw some video footage of people grabbing the snouts of great white sharks as they fed upon a dead whale. Right away I knew that these idiots were liberals. No questions asked. Great whites are Conservatives and for the following reasons. They're at the top of their food chain, always mobile, beautiful and luminous to behold, aggressive and focused when in pursuit of their goals, thick-skinned, and their eyes roll over white during a fight.

These particular geniuses had been aboard boats that had come upon a dead whale. The great whites voraciously fed upon the carcass, which floated both above and below the water's surface. At least one liberal stepped from a boat onto the carcass as the sharks continued to tear chunks from the whale. Another idiot may have even stepped upon the whale while carrying a child.[13]

Every good Conservative understands the value of productive risk. That's why they invest their money in the stock market rather than using it to buy crack, methamphetamine, and lottery tickets. A liberal's idea of risk is that which defies the rules of God, man, and logic. What these people were doing was just plain old liberal D-U-M-B (Democrat Using Minuscule Brain).

Had the sharks pulled the liberals into the ocean and turned them into ground chuck, the subsequent news story would've been *GREAT WHITE SHARK ATTACKS TOURISTS!* This analogy perfectly describes the history of Conservatives and liberals in a nutshell. You figure it out.

LIBERAL SIGHTING #12:

Today I saw a news clip of Barry "The Asterisk" Bonds raising his hands into the air, claiming to have surpassed Babe Ruth's home run record. Other liberals cheered him in his moment of celebrated mediocrity.

Barry … you're no Babe.

LIBERAL SIGHTING #13:

A twenty-two-year-old liberal was charged with stealing an airplane and flying it from Florida to Gwinnett County, Georgia. His father complained to Gwinnett County Sheriff Butch Conway that the poor little thing was apparently developing dental problems in jail because dental floss wasn't allowed there, for obvious reasons. Elder liberal Scott Wolcott claimed that his son, Daniel Andrew Wolcott, could develop gum disease if this barbaric denial of basic liberal rights were allowed to continue.

This wasn't junior Wolcott's first run-in with the law and yet there was good ol' dad, still changing the twenty-two-year-old toddler's poopie diaper.

Sheriff Conway responded like a true Conservative; dutifully, timely, and ingeniously. He moved the accused thief to a new jail cell where his cell-mate was none other than Bart Corbin, a dentist charged with the murder of his wife.[14]

Sheriff Butch Conway, you became one of my personal heroes that day.

LIBERAL SIGHTING #14:

Look for these particular types of liberals, which may be found in any environment:

1. Those who think everyone else in the world should fall madly in love with their imposing and bratty offspring, and who get offended when you don't.

2. Those who think everyone else in the world should fall madly in love with their unleashed pets, and who get offended when you don't.

I wouldn't recommend shooting them unless they're attacking you. Otherwise I suggest calling Animal Control. As for the pets ... whatever your best judgment dictates.

All right. I can't resist the temptation any longer. Let's delve into some more police cases with which I've dealt in my career thus far. These people are just too idiotic to ignore and they're as liberal as they come. These are the people that walk into a voting booth and just look for the D-word.

*** WARNING ***! Some of these liberal actions are quite graphic. I'll do what I can to clean them up a bit, but proceed at your own risk.

LIBERAL SIGHTING #15:

On 07-05-93 a forty-year-old man used his live-in girlfriend's car to go out drinking. She called him and told him to come home and pick her up. He did as she requested and they argued in the car as they drove.

The man waited until his girlfriend wasn't looking as they sat at a red light and he blind-sided her with a punch to the face. They later returned home and the dispute continued until the woman finally called the police.

The man was intoxicated and attempted to fight officers. He was taken into custody and afforded an opportunity to tell his side of the day's events. The most profound statement he could think to make was that the reason we arrested him was simply because he was black.

No, he wasn't from New Orleans, but perhaps he's moved there since then.

LIBERAL SIGHTING #16:

On 07-06-93 a 250-pound truck driver was at an amusement park with his girlfriend and an eleven-year-old boy. The man became furious with the amount of time the boy stood in line to ride one of the water rides, so when the boy finally returned he did what every devout liberal should do. He grabbed the boy by the neck and slammed his head into a fence, and when his girlfriend tried to intervene he punched her in the face twice.

This left wing genius screamed, cussed, spit in the patrol car, and slammed his head into the divider screen on our way to jail.

The reasons that I know he was a hard core liberal was because he was willing to walk over anyone to get what he wanted. Rules and laws didn't apply to him. He was also a liar. He told my partner and I that when we took off his handcuffs he would "kick our asses." If we had a dollar for every time we heard that line, then we wouldn't have to be cops very long before we could retire to tropical island paradises.

LIBERAL SIGHTING #17:

August 23, 1993. An illegal alien in his early twenties was involved in a verbal dispute with his parents and subsequently doused his eleven-year-old sister with gasoline.

The fire department responded to hose down the girl. The police department responded, investigated, and arrested the offender. The man's family members were understandably furious with him.

The case went before a magistrate court judge some weeks later for a probable cause hearing. The family members appeared and lied on behalf of the man to get him out of trouble, including a thoroughly coached eleven-year-old victim. They all now claimed that the girl's being saturated with gasoline had been an accident.

So there sat the judge. *Who do I believe? The police or the family? Hmm. I don't really like the police anyway, so let's go with the family.*

The judge found no probable cause for the arrest and released the offender. I was outraged, since I'd been the arresting officer. The prosecutor on the case happened to be one of the rare ones who actually cared as much about her cases as I did about mine. She was also outraged. Only by forwarding the case to the grand jury did we ultimately get the justice the case deserved.

The liberal judge who threw out the case for the liberal family is now retired and the prosecutor is now a magistrate judge. We're all better off because of both developments.

LIBERAL SIGHTING #18:

Irrefutable evidence that liberals occupy the stupidest levels of the lower human form is all around us. One of their members named Bernard decided to prove the point with great emphasis in November of 1993, when he entered a QuikTrip convenience store to forge a check.

This twenty-nine-year-old rocket scientist of the left came into possession of a blank personal check belonging to a Douglasville, Georgia man whose first name was Steven. Bernard got an ID made by another lefty, bearing his picture and the victim's information from the check. The QT clerk became suspicious of the ID and called the police without Bernard's knowledge, so he was still present when I arrived.

Had Bernard actually paid attention in school, he might have occasionally seen some calligraphic writing. The lower-case V in Steven's name on the check looked sort of like a B because of the calligraphic style of the print. Bernard thought it was a B, so he had his fake ID made bearing the first name "Steben." He would've seen another V in the city name "Douglasville" had he been bright enough to look and he would've known the letters were V's and not B's.

Bernard wasn't bright enough to do that. He maintained his lies that he was "Steben" until we pointed out his ID screw-up. Our calling the real Steven to confirm he'd had some checks stolen was also helpful.

On the way to jail Bernard kept drilling home the fact that he was a branded and card-carrying liberal. The whole thing was suddenly my fault. He was poor and black and I should therefore have pity on him.

"How can you do this to me?" Bernard asked from behind the screen in the patrol car. "It's Thanksgiving."

"They have turkey in prison," I replied.

So Bernard went to jail for felony forgery on Thanksgiving day, 1993. What was the amount of the check he'd forged? That would be $10.03. I always wondered why he hadn't gone for more. I now realize he probably couldn't count any higher.

LIBERAL SIGHTING #19:

Picture this. You're a drunk male named Bart. You currently reside in a camper behind your cousin's house and get into a dispute with family members from the house. The dispute is about your serving the family's five and seven-year-old sons vodka and orange juice. That's also most likely the only kind of screwdriver you know how to handle. Your well-thought-out solution to the family's asking you to leave is to pull out a box cutter and threaten to kill your cousin's husband.

The police are called and they come, investigate, and lock up your narrow little butt. Once you're handcuffed and your ego is safe to run wild, you begin telling the officers what you would do if you weren't handcuffed:

"Ya'll are a bunch of pussies. If I hadn't been handcuffed I'd have knocked the f*** out of that black motherf ... (referring to the back-up officer).

Ya'll sons of bitches."

Being the macho kind of guy you are, your next act is to resist the intake deputies at the jail as they are forced to remove the earring you refused to remove yourself.

You, Big Bad Bart, wind up in physical restraints and threatening God and everyone in his chain of command with lawsuits.

Here's your million-dollar question. Are you:

a) a Conservative?

b) a liberal?

c) a liberal asshole who can't hold his liquor?

LIBERAL SIGHTING #20:

On 07-14-94 at 9:45 p.m. I stopped a pickup truck for running a red light right in front of my patrol car. The thirty-year-old male driver immediately told me his license was "suspended." Not a bad guy so far. At least he was honest about not having a license, but actually he wasn't "suspended." His status was as a "habitual violator," which meant that he'd had several DUI convictions within a five-year period. Getting one DUI conviction through the courts is difficult enough, so getting three within five years isn't a real common occurrence. Catching an HV driving is therefore not an everyday occurrence.

I took him to jail, obtained an arrest warrant, and went home. No big deal. He'd been cooperative, so I'd allowed him to leave the truck in a grocery store parking lot for his wife to retrieve later. This saved them a wrecker bill.

The next afternoon I began my shift as usual by making a loop around my assigned beat. I looked to my left as I passed the grocery store and there was the pickup truck from last night pulling from the parking lot onto the roadway, driven by the same HV from last night.

I stopped him again, arrested him again, and jailed him again. This time I wrote two tickets to his wife, who had driven him to the parking lot to get the truck. She accused me of laying in wait for her husband just so I could catch him driving again.

"Yes, ma'am. I purposely didn't tow your truck so I could hide over there in the bushes for seventeen hours, just banking on the outside chance that your husband could be so dumb as to return to the scene and drive again."

The ingredients of a habitual failure to obey the law and the ability to make wildly idiotic accusations lead to lots of court cases, but they also make for the perfect liberal marriage.

LIBERAL SIGHTING #21:

One chilly Georgia night in January of 1995 I met a liberal named Doug, with whom I would later have a couple of further police-related encounters.

On this particular night he'd been drinking and got into an argument with his wife. This escalated into his collecting his deer rifle and smashing out lights and poking holes into the walls of the mobile home. I arrested Doug and charged him with criminal trespass in connection with the domestic violence law.

So what? you ask.

Oh, I forgot to tell you. This was their wedding day. Not exactly a Conservative American honeymoon. Wouldn't you agree?

LIBERAL SIGHTING #22:

A liberal walks into a bar …

She confronts her boyfriend's ex-girlfriend, shoves her hand down the front of her own pants and says, "Do you want to see what your ex-boyfriend smells like?"

This high-class citizen then withdraws her hand from her pants and wipes it across the other woman's face. The ex-girlfriend takes a swing at her, but the blow is blocked. The instigator then punches the ex-girlfriend in the face and throws a beer on her.

This could just as easily have occurred in the Oval Office in 1998 as it did in Austell, Georgia in 1995. Is there any doubt in either setting that liberals are pigs?

LIBERAL SIGHTING #23:

I had a ride-along with me one evening in July of 1995. He worked for the US Postal Service and had been a graduate of our Civilian Police Academy. We found out as we talked that he worked with the man who would become my father-in-law in two months.

The shift was short on dispatches, which was unusual for evening shift in the southwest portion of the county. I told my ride-along that I would make a pass through the industrial district near the Chattahoochee River, where prostitutes had been known to operate.

I topped a hill in an area through which eighteen-wheelers sometimes passed to pick up or drop off their trailers. There was a burgundy pickup truck at the edge of the roadway and a white male visible to me through the back window of the truck.

The first sign that something was awry was merely the fact that the occupied truck was here. The second sign was that the man in the truck wasn't seated at the wheel. He was centered upon the bench seat.

I approached the truck on foot and peered into the cab. The man still didn't know I was there. Neither did the female whose head was bobbing in his lap.

The two were interrupted, for the sake of ceasing the criminal activity and because I'd just eaten. The man had agreed to pay the woman twenty dollars for the service he'd been receiving. He was married. He owned his own business, had a twenty-dollar bill in one pocket and hundreds in the other. He pleaded to be released. I felt like he'd just made a poor decision and had gotten caught, but I explained to him that it wouldn't be proper to arrest the woman and release him.

The woman was most definitely going to jail. Her name was Marilyn and this *was* her business. She regularly engaged in this activity to pay for the crack that had already claimed all her front teeth. Another trademark was the washcloth she carried, but I'd rather not get detailed about the purpose of that item. Marilyn was more upset about not getting paid than she was about going to jail.

Two years later I was in the process of training a recruit and we pulled into a parking lot near the Chattahoochee River to so some paperwork. A few minutes later I looked up and saw Marilyn walking across the bridge from Atlanta into our county. She was carrying a white washcloth, or at least a washcloth that had once been white.

I called the desk officer at the precinct, gave him Marilyn's name, and requested her date of birth be pulled from our computer system. Her date of birth was relayed to me and I was then able to run an NCIC check on her.

Marilyn saw our police car after she'd crossed the bridge. She did a U-turn and proceeded to return from whence she came. Dispatch advised that there was an outstanding warrant for Marilyn's arrest for failure to appear.

We arrested Marilyn as she crossed the bridge toward Atlanta. She claimed that she'd just been going for a walk. I asked her if the rag in her hand was the same one she'd had when I'd arrested her two years before. Even then she didn't seem quite capable of putting two and two together.

The outstanding warrant was for failure to appear in court on the case I'd made against her in 1995.

This whole thing is quite sad in many ways and humorous in others. Such is law enforcement in general if you stay in it long enough. Such is observing liberal life from day one.

LIBERAL SIGHTING #24:

In the spring of 1996 I was taking a theft report in an apartment complex. A woman drove by and told me she'd heard a gunshot behind her building five minutes earlier and had smelled the burnt powder. I believed her. Any resident of that particular complex would be an expert on the sound and smell of gunfire a week after moving in. I was surprised she hadn't provided the make, model, and caliber of the weapon based on the sound.

I hid near the woman's building and after about ten minutes I saw a male in his mid teens move to the edge of the woods and attempt to fire a handgun at a downward angle. There were several small children of about five or six years of age watching the teen and they were standing between my position and his.

The pistol didn't fire. The boy looked at the weapon, tried to work the slide, and then walked out of sight around the corner of the building. The little children followed him. I couldn't yell at the boy to put down the pistol when I'd first seen him, even though I was behind cover. That might have endangered the children. So I remained silent and followed the group after they rounded the corner.

The teen kept walking, but I saw that the small children had stopped just around the corner of the building. That was good. That got them farther from the armed boy with every step he took.

I was relaying all these pieces of information over my portable radio. I'd requested back-up units respond without sirens and told them where to go.

I rounded the corner of the building and passed the group of little kids. One girl of no more than five followed her in-the-hood training, which often takes place prior to potty training, and she yelled out, "Police! Police!"

"Shut up," I snarled at her. Her eyes got huge, but she didn't yell anymore. All the little kids became as quiet and still as statues. I didn't know until I was later informed by my sergeant that I'd had my radio mike keyed when I'd spoken harshly to the child. My "shut up" had been broadcasted across the entire southern half of the county. Oh, well.

The teen thankfully hadn't heard the little girl's cries of warning and he kept walking away. The last thing I wanted at that moment was him to turn around and begin shooting in our direction.

The boy was about forty yards ahead of me when he finally did notice my presence. He stashed the pistol somewhere around the back porch of one of the apartments and then ran around the corner of that building.

I was also running by that time and radioed the boy's direction and location to responding units. He ran around the corner and was directly met by the twelve-gauge shotgun muzzle of one of my fellow officers, a retired Navy SEAL. He convinced the teen that continuing to run might not be a good idea.

We had to struggle with the boy to get him handcuffed, but no one was injured in the process. I asked the boy what he'd done with the pistol. He wouldn't tell us.

His mother rounded the front corner of the building and began yelling at us.

"That's my son! Why is he in handcuffs? He's a minor! Minors ain't supposed to be handcuffed!"

She refused to listen and kept screaming, so I told her to just leave the area.

"I will!" she hollered. "I'm going to get a lawyer!"

"Fine."

I then turned to her precious angel and again asked him where the pistol was. His mother heard me ask him that and she then turned her wrath where it belonged, upon her son. Two officers had been searching the area for the pistol the boy had hidden and they finally found it in a barbecue grill.

The blue-steel .22 semi-automatic Ruger had a bullet lodged in the rear of the barrel and that had been why it wouldn't fire when I'd first observed the boy. The boy's mother saw the pistol and embarrassment and disappointment flooded her expression.

"Now," I calmly asked her, "do you understand why your 'minor' is in handcuffs?"

She only nodded.

The fifteen-year-old gunslinger was delivered to the county center for youths upon the order of a juvenile court intake officer. He ultimately admitted that the pistol had been passed to him by a drug dealer the day before during a raid at one of the buildings by narcotics agents.

Do liberals learn from their many mistakes? Rarely. Today this guy is twenty-six years old and has moved onto bigger and better crimes. Still a thug. Still a liberal, only now he probably gets to vote.

LIBERAL SIGHTING #25:

Here's a bit of good old fashioned Conservative justice for you. On 09-06-06 a drunk liberal attacked his teenage daughter in their home after she grew tired of his incessant berating and said something back to him.

The family Chihuahua lit into him like a buzz saw and chewed up his hands and feet to the degree that I had to take him to the hospital before going to jail.

The girl was fine. The "man" was also okay, but the dog had to receive a series of shots for exposure to liberalism.

LIBERAL SIGHTING #26:

March, 1997. I was dispatched to a restaurant where two males in their twenties had attempted to depart without paying their $31.24 bill. These weren't just a couple of guys who had forgotten their wallets. Something wasn't quite right about them.

One of them had wandered away to supposedly go to a bank before my arrival. The witnesses said he'd been gone thirty minutes while they stood with the other male. The one who was present when I arrived said his friend had driven them there in a red car, but had gone to a bank to get money.

The male who had supposedly gone to a bank soon returned on foot.

"Where's your car?" I asked him.

"Car? We have no car."

See. Things just weren't quite right with these guys.

They were taken into custody. One of them was wanted on a Georgia warrant and the other provided a false name and date of birth. I found out who he really was at the jail when I conducted a routine search of my patrol car's rear seat and found his Florida Department of Corrections inmate ID card.

"Mr. 'Smith,'" I said to him. "Your name isn't 'Smith.' Turns out your real name is here on this prison ID."

"Smith is my American name," he tried.

Oh, okay. And this incorrect date of birth you gave me at the restaurant … is that your American date of birth?"

No response.

Both were jailed for theft of services and the other offenses mentioned. The magistrate judge gave me a bit of a difficult time about the warrants, asking "what if they really just forgot they had no money on them?"

I explained in more detail and the judge finally approved the warrants with some lingering reluctance. He was trying to afford them the benefit of the doubt and that was his job, so his approach was understandable. Judges also operate on probable cause and don't really like to hear such phrases as *gut instinct*.

A couple of days later I was notified that the two were sought because of a connection to a murder in Florida. A man had supposedly been killed and buried in the sand.

I couldn't get to a phone fast enough to call the magistrate judge and convince him that he'd done the correct thing in approving those warrants. The only thing that could've helped those guys then would've been if their last names had been Kennedy.

So there you have two baker's dozens of liberal sightings in the field. Anyone can spot them and there's no need for binoculars. You can find them at the grocery store, the car wash, the ball game, perhaps even inside your own home. Try keeping a journal of your own liberal sightings for a while. You'll be amazed at how quickly you can fill a book.

10

CONSERVATIVES IN ACTION

I could write a really long chapter about the amazing things Conservatives do. That might end up being long enough to be its own book. This book isn't as much about the terrific aspects of Conservatism as it is about the ridiculousness surrounding liberalism, so I'll keep this chapter short. I just thought it might provide a necessary contrast to the previous chapter.

Conservatives are self-sufficient. They take care of themselves and provide the handouts that liberals receive as our government attempts to play Robin Hood. The difference here is that the government gives to the lazy by robbing the productive; it has nothing to do with being rich.

Conservatives flush. They clean up the socioeconomic crap left by liberals to make our country great. Their job becomes more difficult as time passes, as liberals infiltrate our government branches, schools, and even some of the business world. If liberals had been at the reigns these last 230 years, the United States would look something like Haiti if we even had a country at all. Personally I believe that the liberal mentality wouldn't have had the nuts to even consider drawing a line in the sand for England.

A Conservative would say the twin towers in New York should be built back the same way they were before, right to the last strip of molding. If the sand devils knock them down again, then we build them back again. That's America. Attempting to capture or kill those responsible would of course be part of the process of rebuilding. Moderates claim the area should just be a memorial. Liberals believe that we deserved the attack and they eagerly await the next chance to berate our troops, heckle our President, or cheer the detonation of bombs upon US soil.

Conservatives believe that our laws apply to them as much as every other citizen. That's why you'll find American jails peopled overwhelmingly with liberals and other liberals putting effort into their release. A Conservative pushes for legislation that benefits the country. A liberal pushes for legislation that benefits liberals.

Compare the words and actions of a man like President Ronald Reagan to those of someone like Senator Hillary Clinton. See the respective strength against the weakness, the responsibility versus the irresponsibility, the ability to achieve for the whole rather than pander to society's weak links, and the insistence on stating what he believed instead of her telling some group-of-the-day whatever she thinks they want to hear. This is leadership versus liberalism.

True patriots are out there every day promoting the Conservative cause as a way of life, not just an ideology or a manner of voting. The men and women of every branch of our military come to mind firstly. They're there for all of us and keep us free, even so a left wing prostitute like John Murtha can run his mouth and betray them. Want to stop global warming? Shut Murtha up. That's bound to help by at least one degree globally.

To the members of the US armed forces, thank you! We support and stand behind you!

There are other patriots who immediately come to mind and I'd also like to thank them for the works they seem to tirelessly perform for Conservative America. They are Congressman Tom Price, Senator Saxby Chambliss, Senator Johnny Isakson, Congressman John Linder, Herman Cain, Sean Hannity, Ann Coulter, Michelle Malkin, Neal Boortz, Clark Howard, Michael Savage, and Kim "the Kimmer" Peterson. There are a lot more, but these people have an impact on my life and I wanted to acknowledge them.

I presented a mere twenty-six cases of how liberals behave in real life situations. Now let's take a look at how a few Conservatives handle life.

CONSERVATIVE SIGHTING #1:

A friend of mine moved to a rural region of Georgia years ago when he married. He and his wife were young and wasted little time in starting a family. I was visiting them one weekend when my friend told me that he'd received a letter from some faction of government notifying him that his annual income qualified him to receive vouchers for free milk, bread, cheese, and other items.

He'd laughed at the letter and thrown it away. A Conservative won't accept such things, especially not from the government. A Conservative is smart enough to know that accepting such an offer from government is like borrowing money from a loan shark or taking a free first hit of methamphetamine from a drug dealer. All of them want to get you addicted to their services and keep you coming for more until they own you.

My friend has a good job, built his home in the mountains, and he and his wife have two wonderful daughters. All without the government and their dairy products, thank you very much.

CONSERVATIVE SIGHTING #2:

I always expect a typical liberal reaction from people I confront on my job, especially when I call them to accuse their children of criminal offenses. Once every few years I get to meet an actual *parent* in every sense of the word, beyond the liberal belief that it simply refers to the act of donating or receiving sperm.

I called the mother of a teenage girl to let her know her daughter had been named as a suspect in some harassing telephone calls. The originating phone number was hers, but there was no proof as to the identity of the caller.

The mother's reaction would've been something like this had she been a liberal:

"How dare you accuse *my* child. *My* child wouldn't do that. What evidence do you have? I'll sue. I refuse to answer any further questions. Where's my lawyer?"

That's what I expected. What I received went beyond cooperation. I saw the actions of a true parent. I explained the case to this mother and she called her daughter to the phone. She asked her if she'd made the calls and the girl immediately said no. The mother turned up the verbal heat a notch or two and the girl began to get tongue-tied over the lies she tried to weave together.

"Detective, can I call you back in a few minutes?" the mother said in a stern tone. "I think I can get to the bottom of this."

"Yes, ma'am."

The mother did call me back. She'd obtained the truth from her daughter without having to lay a finger on her. She'd found out her daughter had made the harassing calls and why. She also told me of the punishment that would be inflicted. That she was quite angry at the girl was obvious, not just for making the calls, but then for lying about it.

"What do you need us to do, detective?"

Now it was I who asked permission to call her back in a few minutes. I called the victim and told her about the interaction I'd had with the juvenile and her mother. We discussed the matter briefly.

I called the mother back and informed her that the victim had elected not to prosecute because of the way she was dealing with her daughter and the situation.

I got no arrest statistic because of this handling of the matter, but so what? This is the way all such cases should go. They only result in arrests when the involved parties are liberals. This mother was a beautiful Conservative. For those of you wondering … yes, she was black. Get over it.

CONSERVATIVE SIGHTING #3:

Liberals like to portray Conservatives as miserly penny pinchers, like a bunch of Ebenezer Scrooges running around looking to foreclose on kids' lemonade stands. I love to disappoint liberals, so I'll do so again by telling them that Conservatives define true generosity when it counts.

I'd lost some change from my pocket and was unable to recover it. My eight-year-old daughter saw this happen and said nothing about it at the time. A couple of hours later we were at home and she approached me in my room. She looked at me and asked, "Daddy, were you mad when you lost your money?"

"Well, I wasn't happy about it, but it's not worth getting upset about. It was only a couple of dollars. Why?"

She blinked thoughtfully and took off like a rocket. "I'll be right back," she said.

I already knew what she was doing. I know the kind of child she is and the way she interacts with the people she cares about.

She returned several minutes later with double fistfuls of pennies she'd been collecting and put them atop my dresser. "There you go, Daddy."

She's a child, so she has her liberal moments as she's allowed during her developmental years. Actions like this are purely Conservative, though. I couldn't be more proud of her. My three-year-old has already displayed similar tendencies. Liberalism is a disease, so a possible genetic tendency toward Conservatism cannot be ruled out, either.

I know she's a Conservative in the making because she gave me the pennies and didn't tap into the cash she's collected from the tooth fairy visits mentioned in Chapter Six.

What would a liberal do at this point in this scenario? Hit my daughter with a gift tax on the pennies she gave me and forward the tax to a welfare leech. That's what.

CONSERVATIVE SIGHTING #4:

I've dabbled in the martial arts in the past through classes and readings. I took karate for a couple of years in my late thirties and watched parents bring their kids to the dojo to sign up during that time. I've always found martial artists to be a cut above in every way. The parents want the discipline, exercise, and fun for their children. The kids want the same things for themselves. Yes, dear liberals, children do crave discipline. Some of them don't realize they do at the time, but they certainly are thankful for their instilled discipline later in life.

The majority of children who take martial arts are more respectful of themselves and others than what is the norm. They're also more self-confident and successful at the things they undertake.

So you liberals take a field trip sometime to your local martial arts studios and observe all the little Conservatives in the making. You can probably learn something from them, unless the whole scene is just too barbaric for your liberal palates.

CONSERVATIVE SIGHTING #5:

A police recruit looks to the veterans after which to model his behavior. He selects some to denote behavior he'd like to emulate. He selects others as memorable examples of what *not* to become.

Major Stan Melton is a member of my department and I've known him since he was a sergeant. He was my uniform lieutenant for a year or two after he obtained that promotion and I saw in him much of the attributes I wished to display on the job.

A police officer should be a cut above the average population. Some are and some aren't. I've had the opportunity to be on police calls with fellow officers bearing a broad array of personalities. Some of those calls involved firearms, knives, or other dangers.

I've been on calls like that multiple times with Major Melton. He always handled himself like a true Conservative; honest, confident, level-headed, reasonable, willing and capable of reacting with force if necessary and yet always mindful of appropriate limitations, hoping all the while that matters could be resolved peacefully.

I don't know how the man votes. That's none of my business and definitely not what defines a Conservative. Voting results are incidental to the Conservative lifestyle. The head and the heart are what define a soaring Conservative. Not the polling place.

CONSERVATIVE SIGHTING #6 AND #7:

My parents.

CONSERVATIVE SIGHTING #8:

Police officers take a lot of theft and burglary reports in which victims name their housekeepers as suspects simply due to opportunity. Missing jewelry is a commonly named item in this situation.

I always wondered how much jewelry you could really steal as a housekeeper before a pattern started to develop. There was no way all these housekeepers were stealing everything of which they were suspected. Some of the jewelry reported missing had to either be lost, stolen by someone else, or falsely reported for insurance fraud.

Thirty-five-hundred dollars worth of jewelry was reported stolen from a metro Atlanta area home in June of 2006. The complainant had placed the case of jewelry upon her bed as she prepared to leave on vacation. She later realized that she'd forgotten the case after leaving on a four-day trip to Florida.

The complainant returned home from vacation to discover the case of jewelry was gone and filed a theft report. She mentioned several people who had access to her home while she'd been away. Within a few days the case had been located and returned by the Florida hotel, where the complainant had unknowingly left the case in her room. The cleaning crew at the hotel had found the case and turned it in. Not one piece of jewelry was missing from the case.

A clear conscience is more valuable than jewelry to Conservatives. I know nothing about this cleaning crew other than the fact that this was the act of typical Conservatives, because honesty and integrity are huge factors separating them from the dark side.

CONSERVATIVE SIGHTING #9:

This sighting is dedicated to an entire community! The Georgia city of Kennesaw passed a law in 1982 dictating that residents had to own a firearm and ammunition. Sound crazy? Well, that's what it takes sometimes to combat liberalism. I was in high school then, but I still remember thinking what a stroke of genius and balls it was to pass such a law.

Liberals immediately began screaming about what heinous acts of violence would begin occurring in Kennesaw, Georgia. There would be murder and mayhem galore from border to border within the town. The scene from the OK Corral would be a daily occurrence, unlike the firearm-free paradisiacal environments known to exist in England and New York City.

What Kennesaw got for its effort was a reduction in its crime rate. Imagine that. Burglars and rapists don't want to get shot. Who would've ever thought that to be the case?

The law is still on Kennesaw's books and they continue to enjoy a low crime rate. No sunset duels have reportedly occurred on the town square. Let me be fair, though. There was one subsequent duel that's worth mentioning that happened as a result of this law. The resulting score was Kennesaw 1, the ACLU 0.[15]

Kennesaw ... you rock!

CONSERVATIVE SIGHTING #10:

This sighting is directly linked to the previous. This is tragedy and triumph in just a few paragraphs. True to form, the Conservative element is responsible for the latter.

A liberal bottom-feeder now shovels coal in extreme temperatures as punishment for his September of 2005 crimes. Brian Clark was already a sex offender and rape suspect when he carjacked a thirty-year-old mother, robbed her, shot her, and then crashed her vehicle. She died in the ordeal.

Note the liberal cornerstones of Clark's behavior. The laws didn't apply to him. He was free to do whatever he wanted to do despite prior atrocities, up to and including violating another's life, liberty, and property rights to satisfy his own needs. He needed money, so he simply took it from someone else who had earned it. His thought processes were warped. Oh, and let's not forget his failure to accept accountability by exiting the crashed vehicle and running away. That's a big lib element that can never be overlooked. Clark exited the young woman's vehicle and left her inside dead or soon to be dead. What is it about leaving a woman for dead in a vehicle that's so important to liberals? Is that the official sport of the left?

Enter Shawn Roberts of Kennesaw. He saw what occurred and challenged Clark as he fled the scene. Clark turned to fire in Roberts' direction and was shot dead by Roberts, who just happened to have a firearm of his own. Oh, and Roberts' firearm wasn't stolen. Clark had stolen his from the home of one of his rape victims. Rape ... another staple of liberal life.

There were two unfortunate aspects of this case. One was that the young mother died during the incident. The other was that Roberts' bullet was worth more than Brian Clark, even when Clark had on his pants.

There were also two fortunate outcomes. One was that the Cobb County grand jury didn't indict Shawn Roberts.[16] That should be a given, but get enough libs on a jury and you just never know. Number two is that Clark's forwarding address is now hell instead of a state prison. That's cheaper for us law-abiding tax-payers.

I could've posted this sighting in the previous chapter and focused on the dead liberal criminal. Celebrating his demise is more fun, so my personal thanks are extended to Shawn Roberts.

CONSERVATIVE SIGHTING #11:

To the pilot or pilots who pulled the triggers on Abu Musab al-Zarqawi, you are the surgeons of your trade. Bless you for cutting out that malignant cancer.

CONSERVATIVE SIGHTING #12:

Thomas Autry of Atlanta filleted some liberal pork in May of 2006 during a robbery attempt. He was walking and minding his own business when a pack of teenaged swine attacked him.

These five pigs carried firearms and metal knuckles in their attempt to rob Autry. He tried to escape by running away and dug a pocket knife from his back-pack as he did so. Autry lost the footrace, but won the subsequent struggle by sending one to the morgue, another to the emergency room, and the rest to jail.

The easy target the swine thought they had found was a former US Marine and Gulf War veteran.[17] How much that played in the scenario I don't know. The man was simply trying to defend himself and had obviously switched into survival mode. He was serving his country when these swine were still rooting in their own filth. You know what? Nothing has changed.

CONSERVATIVE SIGHTING #13:

There are a lot of people in this country who work more than one job to make ends meet and to avoid accepting government "assistance." Every one of them deserves our praise for thumbing their noses at the liberal welfare machine.

Support the FairTax bill and remove the claws of the IRS from your own pockets. Who knows? Maybe we could all work one job again.

That baker's dozen should provide enough examples of Conservative behavior to present some glowing differences to the mutts mentioned in Chapter Nine.

I've had both liberal and Conservative friends my entire life. I've valued both. Liberals have their places. Those places simply aren't positions of political power or voting booths. Yes, yes. I know. People are allowed to speak and vote as they choose. This world belongs to all of us, though. The basic truth politically is that Conservatives make the world a better place while liberals bring detriment.

Liberals belong in front of painters' canvases and behind movie cameras (except Michael Moore). Political control is best wielded by the Conservative hand. I default to the analogy of Conservatives being the parents and liberals being the children. Misbehave and we'll spank your little backsides. A liberal will never win an argument with a Conservative as long as we refrain from engaging in debates with them about the MTV Music Awards or the finer techniques of victimizing women.

11

YOU'RE A NATION

That this chapter title sounds very much like a bodily excretion is no accident. Blame my warped sense of humor. One must possess a warped sense of humor to remain in law enforcement as long as I have. If you think I'm warped for this little infraction, then you don't even want to know the kinds of statements made for comic relief at autopsies or homicide scenes. Deal with it.

You're a nation, America. Reality is that we can be one or the other … a nation … or a waste product that was once something terrific. We can be a nation or urination. I'm becoming more convinced as time passes that Conservatives are battling for the former and liberals desperately want to be the latter. Yellow is after all a liberal's favorite color, sometimes being edged aside by a strong affiliation with pink.

Liberals don't flush and they don't wash their hands. They create their own filth and enjoy wallowing in it. Also becoming more obvious as time passes is that neither Republicans nor Democrats are serving Conservative values. So what do we do about this when we see the same old self-serving faces on the ballots?

How wonderful life would be if people could just walk the Earth thinking and acting in that foolishly irresponsible way that liberals have patented. The unfortunate reality is that there are mess-makers and flushers, and America needs Conservatives to clean behind liberals. The flatulence of the left is overwhelming. Frankly though, I'm tired of changing their diapers.

We have buffoons representing us in many levels of government and we keep re-electing them. What does that say about us as a country? The politicians think of us as cattle and we behave accordingly. What happened to men like George Washington? Our forefathers are turning in their graves much the way Mozart and Beethoven do when some idiot spins a "gangsta rap" CD. No, they're not just turning. They're flailing at their coffins. They're disappointed and pissed off! Know what? They have every right to be.

Liberals have their places. Running the country isn't one of them. Most people tend to say things like "both sides should be heard." Perhaps, if the debate is about what color to paint the monkey bars at the park, but the liberal mindset usually seems to make matters worse when used to analyze important domestic and foreign affairs. The liberal mindset works really well the fifteen minutes before you awaken, as the darkness and cobwebs of the dreaming process perform hallucinogenic wonders without all the nasty after-effects of screwing up reality.

Am I suggesting that a liberal's place is in the kitchen, so to speak? Hmm. I guess I am. Our nation, states, and counties seem to chug along just marvelously in the hands of Conservatives, while the opposite is the case with liberals in control. The more liberals that get tossed into the mix, the worse matters typically become. I noticed this when I was in my teens, long before I became good and ornery in wanting to do something about it. I also noticed that some people can call themselves Conservatives and do the correct things, but then backslide before our very eyes and develop liberal tendencies. Liberals are capable of the same movement sometimes, occasionally even displaying backbones and leadership qualities. Too much of those and they would have to turn in their liberal ID cards.

What I find absolutely ridiculous is politicians' attempts to please large groups of people who have special interest motivations. Politicians just don't seem capable of saying no to lobbyists anymore. That would take backbone. Telling people no takes guts. Try these on for size:

"No! I won't approve a tax increase."

"No! I won't support amnesty for illegal aliens."

"No! I won't push for a premature withdrawal from Iraq or the asking of Israel to cease fire."

"No! I won't support the misuse of eminent domain."

"No! I will not sign onto more welfare programs. No! No! No!"

Of course these politicians have their own motivations for pandering to whomever the group of the day might be. They want to keep their jobs and increase their power. They want to scheme so they can sneak favors for those who support and benefit them. A politician with the best of intentions can always become a cancer; a foul and malignant monstrosity that grows and becomes more voracious and destructive with time. Wow. That sounds a lot like so many of the people I've voted *against* these past couple of decades. Perhaps even a few of the ones I've voted *for* as well.

How are you supposed to know who to vote for on election day anymore? Our clear-cut lines have become fuzzy and gray. I used to really enjoy seeing lots of red on an election map and very little blue. Lots of red and little to no blue makes liberals go to their rooms and pout. Red and blue make purple, though, and purple has been clouding my political vision these last five years. Michael Savage was dead on when he used the phrase "Demicans and Republicrats" in *The Political Zoo*.[18] Republicans have been spending like crazy, pushing for amnesty programs for criminals illegally within our borders, and even going so far as to support Louisiana's William Jefferson. Nothing like a little cold hard cash in the ol' freezer, eh Congressman?

I see purple and it's making me very angry. No one represents me anymore for the most part. Folks attend Liberal State University and then go to law school. They become professional manipulators and enter the world of politics, and then they tell us they want to be our representatives. They either do nothing or do the opposite of what they say they will do. The only issue they ever seem to agree upon is when they vote themselves a hefty salary increase. They enter into corruption and scandals as regularly as we run our vehicles through the car wash, and like our vehicles they regularly exit with a film of filth that just won't quite wash off.

Example:

Cynthia McKinney has this very day as I write this escaped criminal charges for her assault on a Capitol Hill police officer. How disgusting. How vile and corrupt. How racist. The message received is that the McKinney farce has legitimized simple battery. I would therefore like to be the first in line to punch her squarely in the nose. Hey, it's a free shot, right? I'll take it. No charges. I'll just wait the newly established waiting period of several months and the grand jury would return no indictment. Right? All I have to do is claim that I'm being unfairly targeted because I'm white and male. Works every time, doesn't it?

Look across our country with a neutral eye for a moment and take notice of the degree of humanity we have as representatives at all levels. Republican, Democrat, or otherwise. How can we possibly view them as our leaders? We shouldn't. How can we count on them? We can't.

The police officers with whom I work are held to a higher standard than many of the thousands of so-called representatives across this nation. An officer who tells one lie will be fired, and yet so many snaky politicians can slither in and out of corruption that we need Harry Potter to interpret their serpentine explanations for us.

Finding an elected official who doesn't have personal gains as a motive for holding his or her position is becoming rare. A lot of them own their own businesses and the elected positions at second glance seem to serve those businesses quite well. The stupid ones get caught. Their chances of going to jail are directly dependent upon how their affiliations match with the current regime. Some are charged. A few even go to jail. Make no mistake, though. These people are aggressive and intelligent, or at least aggressive. They're the meat eaters of white collar and corporate crime. I wouldn't hold my breath waiting for politicians to be held accountable for their wrongdoings.

Why would someone want to sink so much money and effort into obtaining an elected position that may not pay very well, at least atop the table?

"Because I want to serve my community," the politician will answer.

I believe a police officer or soldier who gives that response. A politician? Nope. A politician has to prove to me that his or her motivations are centered around community service or they don't get my vote. They have two to four years to prove themselves and that's plenty. Watch them closely! Don't be part of the voting cattle who simply punch R's and D's. The R's and D's just aren't cutting the mustard lately.

A couple of years ago I had the extreme misfortune of getting assigned a series of cases to investigate that involved the theft or destruction of political campaign signs. I wanted to believe that overzealous citizens were committing the infractions against the opponents of their favorite guys and gals. That wasn't the case.

I talked to at least a half a dozen politicians and political want-to-be types during those ongoing investigations. Rarely have I encountered a group exhibiting more pompousness and unjustifiable arrogance than them.

The media was all over the issue and I really began to question the direction of my career and sense of worth as a detective. I thought to myself, *I'm investigating the theft or toppling of some two-foot pieces of colored cardboard for a bunch of whining and finger-pointing babies.*

I felt like the adult the children run to on the playground hollering, "He's touching me! She's touching me!" The whole ordeal was absolutely unbelievable.

During the investigation it was discovered that many of the signs they were whining about had been planted in locations that violated certain county codes.

Two adult teens were finally arrested one night in the process of stealing campaign signs. The signs in their vehicle belonged to the opponent of the candidate who was paying them. They claimed they were being paid to do exactly what they had been caught doing and there was some evidence to indicate they were telling the truth.

So we threw a big dog and pony show in magistrate court involving lawyers, the teens, witnesses, and of course the political candidates. The other monkey wrench was that the arrest of the teens occurred on the election date, so their candidate had been elected to state office by the time the real fireworks began. That meant a newly elected state senator was very close to being charged with being a party to the crime of theft of colored cardboard.

No one in the court system wanted to touch that case with a ten-foot pole. I didn't really want the thing on my desk either, but when I'm given a case I try to work it fairly and thoroughly. The whole thing came to a head one afternoon as everyone involved appeared before a magistrate judge for an application hearing, otherwise referred to as a pre-arrest hearing. The decision the judge had to make was whether or not there was enough probable cause to arrest the newly elected senator in connection with what his employees had done.

I felt mildly sorry for the arrested teens. I felt like they were decent kids who had been led in the wrong direction not only by their employer, but by their own heads. The father of one of the two was a minister. I felt like he was the only one other than me pressing for the truth rather than some personally-serving variation of it.

The judge jumped at the first opportunity to rid the court of the case and he found no cause for the arrest of the senator-elect.

All of these men and women labeled themselves as Republicans. That may have been so, but these were not the behaviors of true Conservatives. A Conservative doesn't lie and steal. Those tend to be liberal pastimes that should be outgrown by age three.

That whole ordeal left me with several bitter flavors in my mouth. I began to give more serious consideration to the possibility of leaving law enforcement. I began to seriously doubt whether or not we have any truly honest and lionhearted people representing us politically. I began to consider whether or not I myself could enter the world of politics. I still debate with myself over the first two, but the most likely answer to the last would be no.

I wouldn't really want any campaign signs even if I ran for something and it's amazing how many idiotic voters base their decisions on something so meaningless. I wouldn't want to engage in the negativity and mud-slinging that encompasses most modern elections. My attitude would be, "Here I am. Here's what I've done and here's what I want to do. Vote for me if you agree. Vote for my opponent if you don't." Can a candidate get away with such honesty in modern politics? Probably not.

The state senator from the scenario above went on to present an immigration bill that proposed to make things tougher on illegal aliens and it passed. That part of the story is terrific. I say the tougher the better. I'll still never quite be able to shake my earlier image of him seated across from me in our interview/interrogation room with his attorney at his side, selectively answering questions related to the arrests of his campaign assistants. That's not the image any American citizen should have of their so-called "leaders." Not our President. Not our US or state congressional or senatorial reps. Not our county boards or city councils. Frankly I'd expect better from the custodians in our schools, and do you know what? Many of them probably are.

All of this sounds really bleak, this woeful view of our elected officials and government. Things are rarely as bad as they appear, even in this case. The bad news is that you often have very little from which to choose on a ballot, like you're having to choose between scorpions and spiders.

The good news is that if you and enough people like you demand something better for yourselves and your communities, you can use the power of your vote to shuffle out the bad eggs as soon as possible. Time and attrition will wash out the filth. Don't clean house like that and you get what you deserve, such as someone like Cynthia McKinney. Yes! You, Cynthia! You hear me talking, woman? You're despicable! Your district is a political landfill where *you're a nation* becomes *urination!*

We had all better do something if we expect this good ride called America to continue. The monster we call government is far too large and totally out of control in its quest to be totally in control. The monster steals our money and calls it taxes. The monster steals our property and grunts, "Eminent domain." This monster hikes its leg on the Statue of Liberty and takes regular steaming dumps on the Constitution. "Living Constitution," indeed. There are some leeches attached to the monstrous host who call themselves representatives, who actually sympathize with the Middle Eastern sand devils who want to destroy us. This will not do. Good people (you know … Conservatives) can only take so much before they switch to survival mode. We're not there yet. Not even close, thank goodness. I'll tell you shortly what happens when that point is reached, but brace yourself because it's not pretty.

You're a nation, America. Now hear this! YOU'RE A REPUBLIC! That means we don't concern ourselves with the concept of social equality. This isn't a dictatorship, despite what some Democrats try to do. No one is oppressed unless they oppress themselves. You hear that, Jesse? Al? Social equality calls for a manipulated and manipulative society of mediocrities who seek to punish initiative and lift up laziness. You're a republic, America. We all have the same opportunities even though we're born into varying circumstances. The richest child may wind up a bum. The poorest child may work his way to riches. The possibilities are endless and exciting.

The one huge ingredient that's not part of our republic that liberals keep wanting to stir into the mix is *government intervention in every aspect of our lives.* That's not part of a republic. That level of government intervention makes for a really good communist dictatorship, otherwise referred to as urination.

Wake up, America. You're in the middle of a war and you're doing a good job against the enemy, but there is an enemy right here at home. Liberals! People are either for or against the United States. Liberals have clearly stated their case over and over that they are very much against this nation. They don't fight our nation with weapons of war, although many of them support those who do. Liberals battle the United States by trying to overthrow her from within, to change her into the abomination they desire her to be.

Most people believe in the concepts of good and evil. There's no way to coat this statement with sugar. Liberals are evil! Anyone who seeks to undo all for which the men and women before us have so honorably fought and died is the enemy. My tolerance for free speech stops with being subjected to listening to blasphemies against this nation by a class of cartilage-framed communists known as liberals.

I've often wondered why liberals don't leave the United States since they hate her so much. Why don't they renounce their citizenship and go live in whatever second or third world country best suits their pink palates? The answer is that they don't have the guts to live in those places.

Has-been movie actor and failed talk show host Alec Baldwin said he was moving to France years ago. Hey, Alec! We're still waiting! Go over there and see what President Chirac does to protect you from the violent Muslims that will burn your car and stuff your head with cheese. Baldwin won't go because he knows that Chirac has more estrogen than President Bush does testosterone, and that's a fair amount in either case.

Not all liberals are of course so radical. Many of them genuinely want good things for the United States. Their methods and intentions do work in some circumstances. You simply can't establish and operate a strong nation on their principles, though. Maybe I see this so clearly because of my job as a police officer. Maintaining a strong and benevolent nation of people is like being a cop. We must be capable and willing to use that force necessary to ensure peace and freedom, hoping and praying that no loss of innocent life occurs in the process.

Be a police officer for a moment. Let's work a domestic dispute like a Conservative and then like a liberal. Look for the analogies of running a nation as we proceed.

FIRST SCENARIO:

You're Officer I.M. Right. You respond to the home of John and Jane Lawless on a domestic dispute. John is growling mad, frothing at the mouth, and nursing his left hand. He tells you to leave because this is his house and you have no right to be here. You ask John what happened and he says he and Jane just got into an argument. "No big deal."

"What happened to your hand?" you ask him.

"I held it up to defend myself and Jane hit it with her face."

Now you ask the crying Jane Lawless what happened as you take notice of her swollen right eye.

"John and I got into an argument and he punched me in the face."

You arrest John Lawless for domestic violence and charge him with battery against Jane.

"Wait!" John yells as you cuff him. "Give me another chance! I'll do better!"

"Uh … no."

SECOND SCENARIO:

You're Officer I.M. Left. You respond to the house of John and Jane Lawless on a domestic dispute. This is the third time you've been to their house in as many days. Two days ago John had slapped Jane in the face, according to Jane. Sure his palm had been as red as her cheek, but he'd said that had been because she'd caught him in a "private moment." His redness had been from the act and hers from the embarrassment of catching him in that act. So she'd only been embarrassed on the right side of her face. Hey, it could happen, right?

Yesterday Jane called again and you responded to find John growling mad, frothing at the mouth, and nursing his left hand. He told you to leave because this was his house and you had no right to be there. You decided John was probably correct about that and turned to leave.

"Wait!" called out the crying Jane Lawless. "He punched me in the face!"

You turned to John Lawless, who said, "Bull hockey! I held up my fist like this here to defend myself from her charge and she ran into it with her face."

That could happen, you decided. That would explain Jane's swollen right eye.

"Give us another chance," John told you with his big green grin. "We'll do better."

"Uh … okay."

Today you don't have to knock, because the door is splintered off the hinges. There are holes in the walls framed in blood and broken pictures upon the floor.

You enter the living room and the first thing you see is John holding down Jane and punching her repeatedly.

What drove poor John to this point, you wonder. Did Jane do something to deserve his wrath?

"Make him stop!" hollers Jane Lawless.

John Lawless protests. "This is *my* house. This is *my* wife. You have no authority to be here, so leave."

"Okay, but first I'd like to ask you to stop pounding Jane's face. You're getting blood everywhere and the EPA won't like that. You're also obviously very angry and that's contributing to global warming."

"Huh? You kiddin' me?"

You reach into one of the pouches on your dry-rotted gun belt and withdraw your stun gun. You hand it to John. "Here. Use this on Jane instead. It's environmentally friendly and you won't hurt your hand anymore."

With that you leave, Officer I.M. Left. Tomorrow is your off day, but Officer I.M. Right will respond to this location to work the homicide of Jane at the hands of John.

"Well," you'll later state, "Jane would still be alive if Officer Right had done his job."

So what do you think of this wild analogy? I unfortunately think it's not nearly as wild as some of the dastardly things liberals have done to our nation and the world.

That brings me to my next topic, which is a favorite of liberals and Conservatives alike, but for very different reasons. WAR. History has shown countless times that people are power-hungry creatures and will ultimately rely upon war to resolve their brewing differences. We can't help it. Men have the drive to want to kill one another. Welcome to nature. More women seem to want to join the reindeer games as time continues. Are we doomed? Probably. Definitely if we follow liberals. The only chance I give our species is if Conservatives are at the helm without liberal interference. Show me that utopian nation and I'll show you some tropical resorts in the Antarctic Circle.

Liberals whine that we have no business involving our military in foreign conflicts. Hey, idiots! We took that approach in the years leading to WWII, and if it hadn't been for the awesome work and sacrifices of the Allied Forces we would be speaking German right now. You wouldn't get to present your asinine arguments over flag issues because they would all be the same red, black, and white with the twisted cross.

Our twenty-first century Pearl Harbor occurred on 9/11. One difference is that CNN didn't have its distorted camera lens in the middle of the WWII action or fiction writers posing as reporters. We also didn't have John Murtha contributing to the efforts of the enemy by being a traitor. He would've been thumped like a fly if he'd done so then.

Despite the fact that George W. Bush is failing us on the immigration issue, he's our supreme leader on the current war effort against the sand devils of the Middle East. I personally couldn't be more proud of him for sticking to the fight. He has to not only face the responsibility of heading the fight against the terrorists of extreme Islam, he has bloated pencil-pushing terrorist sympathizers ridiculing him from within our own government. Allow me to be blunt. Every one of them should be taken out and shot like the traitors they are. US Representative brand bacon is far too fatty for human consumption when the swine have fed upon a steady diet of liberalism and treason, but it's suitable for serving to dogs.

President George W. Bush is a human being. You liberals out there in fantasy land would instantly crumble under the pressure that man has to bear in his waking *and* sleeping hours. He's the one holding us together right now. I cringe when I consider where we might be as a nation right now had Al Gore or John Kerry been handed the reins. If they had a responsible brain between them then they would take it out and shoot marbles with it. Not all evil is genius. That's only in the movies.

America, you're a free nation because of the strength of the skeletal structure your forefathers designed into you. That strength has been maintained by multiple things including war, fought so bravely by the personnel of our armed forces.

Some liberal lawyer scoops up enough money and support to convince the voting cattle of his district that they should vote for him. Then that lawyer heads to Washington wearing the title of US representative only to ridicule our President, military, and nation. Who are they and what gives them the right to do that? Each one is not merely a disgrace, but is a hemorrhoid upon the anus of government. I will not allow those types to soil the red carpet heritage placed before us by the men and women of the US Military. So what do we say of the John Murthas and John Kerrys who claim to be veterans and then speak with the forked tongues of traitors? Simple. View them as the traitors they are and renounce them. If they're not for us, then they're the enemy just as sure as if they wore sandals and carried AK-47's. Murtha is a false hero and Kerry isn't even that. He's a false veteran.

War must be horrible. I cannot speak about that firsthand. The closest I've been to war is as a police officer, punching a car thief who wanted to fight, nearly having to shoot a man on a domestic dispute on Christmas eve, responding to the scene of the shooting of three of our own officers, gazing upon a murdered four-year-old, etcetera. These things pale in comparison to the scenes upon a true battlefield.

Today I took my eight-year-old daughter to walk one of the trails at Kennesaw Mountain National Battlefield Park. She loves to go there because of the wide open space that has become so rare in our country. She likes to look at the wildflowers and wildlife. Today I showed her some trenches that are still in place where Confederate soldiers had dug themselves in. The trenches are situated atop a steep hill overlooking a field in the middle ground and woods in the background. About a hundred feet from the trench nearest the rim of the peak there's a tunnel entrance only a couple of feet wide. That entrance has been shored with marble to preserve some of the structural integrity.

The tunnel had been started by Union troops and its purpose was to allow them to burrow beneath the Confederates entrenched above and blow them up. Two cannons surrounded by mounded earth overlook the entire scene. The battle ended before the use of the tunnel became necessary.

I tried explaining what had happened there 150 years ago to my daughter, but she just couldn't comprehend the idea that American men had done such things to one another. She was more concerned with a fuzzy tan caterpillar that was crossing her path. She can't comprehend the fact that the KFC Big Chicken wasn't present in 1865. She's eight. She has a right to have such a carefree approach. That right has been fought for and won numerous times by men willing to go the lengths as those atop that ridge 150 years ago. Do you think eight-year-old girls in Iraq have ever been afforded the same outlook? The men and women of our armed forces now work to give them that chance while at the same time insuring a more secure United States of America. How dare anyone call himself an American and berate our troops? This is our nation, America. In the words of Herman Cain, "Get on board or get out of the way!"

I'd like to think that all nations could just drop their weapons and work together in positive directions. That will never be possible on this Earth as we know it as long as there is one power-hungry tyrant without a conscience, one liberal willing to placate him, and one Conservative unwilling to tolerate either. I'm no professional political analyst, but I'm extremely thankful to have developed the heart and mind of the latter. Choose your side, because the first two worms are on the same team.

So what does the future hold for our United States ... a strong nation or a rancid yellow puddle? That depends on the outcome of the war.

War? Oh my God! What war? No, I'm not talking about the Middle East. I'm referring to the war that's building right here within our own borders between Conservatism and liberalism. Now you ask me, "Surely you're not suggesting that an actual *war* will take place, are you? Another American *civil war?*"

I lean toward your face with its dangling jaw and wide eyes to state, "That's exactly what I'm suggesting."

There are too many issues on the table not being resolved and too many tempers rising. That's what I meant when I said that people can only take so much before they snap and the results will not be pretty. Americans will eventually be fighting one another in the streets unless everything takes a serious upward turn in coming years.

We're being invaded by Mexico and little has been done to stop that. Politicians in Washington can't even agree on a method to do so. The American tax system is nothing but a gargantuan criminal enterprise and aside from a few people like John Linder, nothing is being done to squash it. Americans are divided on many issues of the war in Iraq. Our courts no longer function properly because there are more problems than solutions. Most of our public schools suck. Most of the universities are infested with liberal-minded fire ants, or should I say piss ants? We oppose one another on many environmental issues. We adamantly disagree on the federal handling of the hurricane Katrina aftereffects. The left says Hillary Clinton would make a wonderful President, when we would probably be better off with Hilary Duff. At least Lizzie McGuire is well principled. Her ankles look better, too.

Maintaining your inner child is terrific. I'm all for that. The point is that the little lib inside you should stick to being awestruck by caterpillars rather than initiating policy and instigating our sure annihilation.

What's the answer to avoiding Civil War Part II; The Sequel? I don't think I have one for you on our current course. The war 150 years ago was fought north to south and for very different reasons than the multiple problems now brewing. George W. Bush didn't start the problems and he most certainly won't be in office to see most of them to fruition. He simply inherited them and will pass them on, but in a different format. The civil war I see coming will be north to south *and* east to west. I also believe that conflicts will occur chaotically and not with the honor of the regiments of the 1860's. All I can say is that I hope I'm wrong, and if so then history would've run afoul of its patterns.

How far out will this war be? If things keep heating up like they have been, then I'd guess somewhere between twenty to fifty years. Maybe sooner if things take a dramatic turn. Maybe longer if circumstances cool somewhat in the meantime. We simply can't have the population of this nation increasing at the rate it has been when so many of those people are causing so many problems and not expect inevitable violence. I've only developed these ideas within the last few years that civil unrest is headed our way. Gut instinct is a different concept to explain on a witness stand as a police officer. Officers commonly use the phrase "in my training and experience" to explain a lot of their actions to juries and judges, but gut instinct can be a part of the meaning behind that phrase. Why do I think civil war is in our future on the present course? Call it gut instinct.

Liberals are supposedly breeding faster than Conservatives and that means the criminals will eventually outnumber the law-abiding citizens. As a Conservative that doesn't mean I'm doomed; it just means that I need to store more ammo.

A soldier is endlessly thankful for good food and shelter after being deprived of these long enough. Perhaps liberals would be more thankful for freedom if they were denied its benefits for a while, so get out! Move to the countries you support so much. Post your comments in the French newspapers rather than *USA Today.*

I've always found it amazing that liberals point their fingers at Conservatives and call them warmongers, when liberals have traditionally been the cause of war. They're just too ignorant to see that and are incapable of learning from their mistakes. An all Conservative world would enjoy peace and prosperity. An all liberal world would be in total chaos. Throw the two together and you get the tug-of-war we have in America right now. Who will win? I guess we'll find out, won't we?

Many complain about the polarization of America. I was in agreement with that complaint until recently. I've changed my mind. The polarization will leave little doubt about which side people are on when and if the time arrives to actually fight the civil war liberals are promoting. I just want to know the colors of their uniforms and flags so I'll know what to engage. I predict pink and yellow with rainbow patches.

The Conservative is the hawk that soars above the field of honor, capitalism, and strength. The liberal is the crow that follows the hawk, squawking, flapping wildly, and diving at the superior bird. That hawk puts up with the nuisance and interference for a while. The hawk ultimately turns and grabs the crow, sinks in its talons, and throws the refuse to the ground.

The hawk lands beside the mass, his head high with majestic confidence, knowing that this is the only kind of crow he will ever have to eat.

12

HOPE

A Conservative tends to be an optimist even after being critical, so I repressed the need to call this final chapter "Hopelessness." I'll search for a few good things to say about liberals. That means this will be the shortest chapter due to lack of material. Liberals don't flush, but I'll try to say a few nice things for the purpose of ending on an optimistic note.

Liberalism doesn't necessarily make for bad people, just extremely bad politicians and constituents. There really is hope for some liberals as long as they're not part of the criminal element of America. To hell with the criminals.

The finest liberals I've ever met live in my home. Their ages are three and eight. The world is wondrous to my daughters right now and rightfully so. They won't be liberals for long, because they've already developed very respectable senses of right and wrong (hey, a liberal rhyme). They're still allowed to analyze the world around them with humorously uninformed minds and report on their findings without being referred to as biased. Everyone tells a parent to "enjoy these times now, because they grow up so quickly." My daughters need not worry about growing up too quickly, but grow up they will. The torch of Conservatism will be passed along.

I've read that Steven Spielberg and Tom Hanks are two of Hollywood's liberals. That may be. I don't know their affiliations or specific ideas, but I do know that they labored in the production of two of the finest WWII films ever made. One was *Saving Private Ryan* and the other was *Band of Brothers*. Both were masterpieces and it's difficult for me to comprehend that liberals were behind them. A liberal typically takes a piece of history and skews it to suit his modern belief system. That's not the case with these Spielberg films. I don't see how anyone could watch those stories unfold and not be left with an overwhelming sense of patriotism regarding the American soldier and the United States. I liked both films despite the depressing element of war and death.

Spielberg is responsible for some of my favorite films anyway. *Jaws* is my favorite film of all time. Others were *Close Encounters of the Third Kind, Raiders of the Lost Ark,* and *Jurassic Park. Schindler's List* is a picture everyone should see at least once, but have some Kleenex on hand. I've seen it three times. The little girl in the red coat is a character I will never forget and that's a good thing. Not forgetting is the reason for watching the film in the first place.

Conservatives rightfully hammer the government school system as liberal basic training camps. I do know of some dedicated Conservative teachers who don't fit into that mold, though. They obtained education degrees because they wanted to work with kids and help them learn properly. Those select few didn't design their screwed up system anymore than I did the criminal injustice system. They do what I do, which is the best they can with that which they're presented. I applaud them. Teaching the modern youth is not easy.

Not all liberals are lazy. Some are quite productive at making very nice pieces of pottery, tie-dyed shirts, bird houses, and paintings of rainbows. They can make a respectable living selling these things at county fairs or street corners, but the same should never be attempted on the floor of the House or Senate.

I've found the females of the liberal species to be quite friendly and helpful when they're employed within the national parks of the US. You see? Even I am willing to admit that liberals can be successful in government work under the correct circumstances.

Most of the liberals I know are passive. I'm willing to engage in discussions with them about politics, religion or whatever, but I've found that they tend to want to change the subject momentarily after hearing something they really don't want to hear. I don't fault them for that. What's the point in continuing a game of checkers when your opponent is simply fleeing about the board with his final piece? The point is that I haven't been able to find a liberal capable of going for the throat like some of those shown on the national news channels. I've found liberals to be peacefully within their trademark mental fog and I guess that explains why most of them don't want to make a habit of attacking Conservatives.

Let's see. What else?

Uhhh ...

◆   ◆   ◆

Well I guess that's about all I can muster for this chapter. Sorry I couldn't think of more positive comments about the left. I don't believe I've forgotten anything. There just isn't anything else.

Many changes have occurred just in the few months I spent writing this material. Some changes have been good. Cynthia McKinney was voted out, for example. Other changes are not so good. Democrats gained control of both Houses because Republicans have been so ineffective. Race baiters have been bellowing louder than ever about any issue they see as an opportunity to make money and more powerful names for themselves. Liberal politicians continue to speak with traitors' tongues about our country, our President, and our military. The big picture leaves me with an intense feeling of hopelessness. The names being discussed as potential presidential candidates for 2008 only serve to expand the hopelessness.

The good news is that Conservatives tend to be extremely resilient and strong. I truly hope for all our sakes that these characteristics can be effectively exercised at the polling places rather than in the streets of America. In either arena ... liberalism must be flushed if freedom is to survive.

My conscious mind has been troubled by all these issues in recent years and that's what led to the production of this book. The following is evidence that my subconscious mind is not only working overtime to relieve some of the pressure, but with an occasional sense of humor in so doing. Best wishes.

I had a dream about a month ago that Ted Kennedy died. Mary Jo Kopechne was granted a temporary visa from her eternal resting place to ferry him across the river Styx.

"Sorry about that little *thing* back then," he said with a grin.

She only glared at him and kept the ferry moving.

He looked around with increased horror and said with a shaky voice, "I never thought this place was real."

"Don't worry, Senator," Mary Jo replied. "You won't be alone. Your friends are legion here." There was a long silence between them, other than the moving of the water and the distant screams. She finally broke the silence as the opposite shore and creatures upon it drew near. "So, Senator ... how's the party?"

"It died," he mumbled as his head drooped. "The party died."

NOTES

CHAPTER 3

1. John H. Fund, "Taliban Man at Yale," *The Wall Street Journal*, March 23, 2006.

CHAPTER 5

2. *The American Heritage Dictionary*, Second College Edition (Boston: Houghton Mifflin Company, 1985).

CHAPTER 6

3. Neal Boortz and Congressman John Linder, *The FairTax Book* (New York: Regan Books, 2005), pp. 81-85.

CHAPTER 7

4. Staff and wire reports, "Astros First Series Team Since '53 Without Black Player," *USA Today*, October 26, 2005.

5. David Simpson, Mae Gentry, and Ernie Suggs, "Jones Meets with Police Officials after Graham's Resignation," *The Atlanta Journal-Constitution*, May 4, 2006, http://www.ajc.com/newscontent/metro/dekalb/stories/0504metdekalb.html.

CHAPTER 8

6. Bill Cosby, "The Grandparents," *Bill Cosby: Himself* (Motown Record Corporation, 1982).

7. "US Senate Roll Call Votes 109th Congress-2nd Session," www.senate.gov, May 16, 2006, http://www.senate.gov/legislative/LIS/roll_call_lists/roll_call_vote_cfm.cfm?congress=109&session=2&vote=00121.

8.   Brian Whitman, interview with Sean Hannity, Mark Levin, and Alec Baldwin, "The Brian Whitman Show," News Talk Radio 77 WABC-AM (New York), March 26, 2006.

9.   "Andy Discovers America," *The Andy Griffith Show* (Mayberry Enterprises, 1963).

10.   *The Karate Kid* (Columbia Pictures, 1984).

CHAPTER 9

11.   "Cynthia McKinney & Buckwheat: Separated at Birth?" www.Strange Politics.com, http://www.strangepolitics.com/content/item/115223.html.

12.   "Feds: Lawmaker Hid Bribe In Freezer," www.cbsnews.com, May 21, 2006, http://www.cbsnews.com/stories/2006/05/21/politics/main1638404.shtml.

13.   "Shark Frenzy Tourists Madden Minister," www.theexplodingwhale.com, July 25, 2001, http://www.theexplodingwhale.com/more-whales/20010731-australia/.

14.   Rick Badie, "Jet-Setting Life Can Lead to Gum Decay," *The Atlanta Journal-Constitution*, March 2, 2006, http://www.ajc.com/metro/content/sharedblogs/ajc/badie/entries/2006/03/02/jetsetting_life.html.

CHAPTER 10

15.   Jonathan Hamilton and David Burch, "Gun Ownership-It's The Law In Kennesaw," *Marietta Daily Journal*, March 11, 2001.

16.   "Man Who Killed Carjacker Cleared," *The Associated Press*, 11Alive.com, April 18, 2006, http://www.11alive.com/news/news_article.aspx?storyid=78720.

17.   "Ex-Marine Apologizes For Killing Robbery Suspect," *The Associated Press*, WSBTV.com, May 31, 2006, http://www.wsbtv.com/news/9290011/detail.html.

CHAPTER 11

18. Michael Savage, *The Political Zoo* (Nashville: Nelson Current, 2006), p. 105.

978-0-595-42419-1
0-595-42419-8

www.ingramcontent.com/pod-product-compliance
Lightning Source LLC
Chambersburg PA
CBHW051421280526
45785CB00003B/1115